P9-DEP-052

Beyond Liberation

The Gospel in the Black American Experience

Carl F. Ellis, Jr.

InterVarsity Press
Downers Grove
Illinois 60515

© 1983 by Inter-Varsity Christian Fellowship of the United States of America

All rights reserved. No part of this book may be reproduced in any form without written permission from InterVarsity Press, Downers Grove, Illinois.

InterVarsity Press is the book-publishing division of Inter-Varsity Christian Fellowship, a student movement active on campus at hundreds of universities, colleges and schools of nursing. For information about local and regional activities, write IVCF, 233 Langdon St., Madison, WI 53703.

Distributed in Canada through InterVarsity Press, 860 Denison St., Unit 3, Markham. Ontario L3R 4H1, Canada.

Acknowledgment is made to the following for the use of copyrighted material:

All Scripture quotations, unless otherwise indicated, are from the Holy Bible: New International Version, copyright © 1978 by the New York International Bible Society. Used by permission of Zondervan Bible Publishers.

All Scripture quotations marked RSV are from the Revised Standard Version of the Bible, copyrighted 1946, 1952, © 1971, 1973.

Specified excerpts totaling approximately 1450 words from Stride toward Freedom: the Montgomery Story by Martin Luther King, Jr. Copyright © 1958 by Martin Luther King, Jr. Reprinted by permission of Harper & Row, Publishers, Inc.

Specified excerpts totaling approximately 1250 words from Why We Can't Wait by Martin Luther King, Jr. Copyright © 1963, 1964 by Martin Luther King, Jr. Reprinted by permission of Harper & Row Publishers, Inc.

Much of the material on Malcolm X is from The Autobiography of Malcom X, by Malcolm X with Alex Haley. Copyright © 1964 by Alex Haley and Malcolm X. Copyright © 1965 by Alex Haley and Betty Shabazz. Reprinted by permission of Random House, Inc.

The poem by James Weldon Johnson quoted in chapter fifteen is "Lift Every Voice and Sing" © Copyright: Edward B. Marks Music Corporation. Used by permission.

Cover photographs of Martin Luther King, Jr., and Malcolm X: Wide World Photos.

Cover photographs of Frederick Douglass, Harriet Tubman, Booker T. Washington and W. E. B. DuBois: Historical Pictures Service, Chicago.

ISBN 0-87784-914-5

Printed in the United States of America

Library of Congress Cataloging in Publication Data

Ellis, Carl F., 1946-
  Beyond liberation.

  Includes bibliographical references.
  1. Afro-Americans–Religion. I. Title.
BR563.N4E44   1983   208'.996073   83-18561
ISBN 0-87784-914-5

| 18 | 17 | 16 | 15 | 14 | 13 | 12 | 11 | 10 | 9 | 8 | 7 | 6 | 5 | 4 | 3 | 2 | 1 |
| 95 | 94 | 93 | 92 | 91 | 90 | 89 | 88 | 87 | 86 | 85 | 84 | 83 | | | | | |

LINCOLN CHRISTIAN COLLEGE AND SEMINARY

To Edwina and to Carl III

101214

Acknowledgments

This book would never have been conceived or written without the influence of significant people in my life. To them I will always be grateful.

From the day I was born to Carl F. Ellis, Sr., and his lovely wife, Mildred, I was raised to feel loved and wanted in more ways than I can count. They took great care to supervise my development, exposing me to a rich variety of learning experiences and challenging me to think things through. I will never be able to fully express my loving gratitude to them.

Also I want to thank others whose positive influence is still felt and appreciated. Among them: Catherine Owens (my maternal grandmother) whose example of godliness inspired me to seek God with all my heart; "Uncle James" (James McLain) whose affectionate love for God and for me has been a great source of strength, along with his wife, Blanch (my paternal grandmother), who instilled in me the assurance that being Black should never block me from doing what I set my mind to; Dr. Martin Luther King, Jr., who opened my eyes to God's concern for justice and equality among people; Malcolm X who sensitized me to the beauty of Black humanity; the Reverend Robert Lowery who showed me through his example that the pastoral ministry can be "peopley" and practical; Robert Sykes and Gerald Garnett who took time to share their faith with me, answering my intellectual questions and leading me to Christ; Robert Crowe (my high-school math and science teacher) who relentlessly challenged my new faith, driving me to develop sound reasons for the hope that was in me; Eric Fife whom God used to call me into the ministry; Dr. Clark Pinnock who first helped me appreciate how the truths of Christianity could successfully confront the philosophies of men; Dr. Francis Schaeffer whose insights and writings equipped me to think in terms of a Christian world and life view; Tom Skinner whose ministry has done a great deal to build a platform for the emergence of a new national Black Christian movement; Dr. William Pannell (my supervisor while I worked with Tom Skinner Associates, TSA) whose brilliant insights and feedback contributed much to clarify my theology; my other TSA coworkers including Roland Tisdale, Richard Parker, Henry Greenidge, Eric Payne and Curtis Goffe, whose fellowship and friendship have meant so much to me; the Reverend Richard Woodward whose teaching ministry was a great encouragement in a time of discouragement; Dr. Columbus Salley who provided the tools I needed to integrate my Blackness with my Christian commitment; the Reverend Orlando Protho (my stepfather) who ordained me and whose enlightenment enabled me to appreciate the Black church and Black preaching in a new way; Thom Hopler whose impact on me was limited only by the brief time we had to share; all my professors at Westminster Theological Seminary (WTS) who helped to further clarify my thinking, especially Dr. John Frame, Dr. Harvie Conn, Dr. Robert Knudson and Bill Krispin (director of the center for Urban Theological Studies); the Reverend Bill Link (dean at WTS); whose personal concern and financial sacrifice enabled me to enroll at WTS; the brothers and sisters in the "West Philly" (Philadelphia) group whose fellowship and warmth carried me through the difficult days of my senior year at seminary; Prison Fellowship which gave me, as a seminar instructor, a means of digesting the heavy things I learned at WTS; New City Fellowship which provided me, as pastor, an opportunity to implement some of the things I have written about; Inter-Varsity Christian Fellowship which brought me into contact with many of the influential people in my life; and, finally, my beloved son, "Franky," born June 8, 1983, who gave me breaks from my workaholism by pleading to be held, then batting the papers of my manuscript off the table while drooling on the ones that were left.

Next I want to thank all those who did the typing, retyping, editing, re-editing and so on. They include: Isidra Smith; Carla Walters; Michelle Black; Lesley Hamilton; Pat Holland; Catherine Nordlof; Lunard and Sharon Lewis; David and Arlene Cadwell; Daniel Bockert; Mrs. Mildred Protho (my mother); E. Regina Elliott (my foxy sister-in-law); Joan Guest, Jane Wells and the rest of the staff of InterVarsity Press; Mark Branson, Bob Hunter, Dr. Bennie Goodwin and others who reviewed the manuscript and gave many helpful suggestions.

And finally thanks to Edwina Elliott Ellis who gave me much encouragement, was my sounding board and best critic, and put up with me during the long hours I spent in the writing of this book.

Most of all I want to give thanks to my heavenly Father whose amazing grace made all this possible.

Chapter 1

Toward a
Promised Land

FOR FOUR HUNDRED YEARS they had been oppressed. Their sense
of history and destiny was all but wiped out. Their consciousness
was blurred and distorted, their culture polluted with false values.
Their knowledge of the one true God had been outgunned by a proliferation of manmade gods. Their sense of dignity had been over-
whelmed by feelings of inferiority, feelings which came from the
dehumanization inflicted by a racist society.

The people felt forsaken by God. Yet God remained faithful. He
did not forsake them. In fact, he was already implementing his
eternal plan of liberation. In ten demonstrations of judgment, God
broke the back of a king who had used his technology to maintain

a brutal system of slavery. God thus brought his people out of Egypt so that they might become his light to the nations.

This goal, however, could not be reached overnight. The people had to be prepared slowly through de-Egyptianization as they journeyed in the wilderness. God began to restore their culture, raising it to new heights through Moses and the law.

Parallels in History

A survey of Black history reveals that, like the children of Israel, we have had a four-hundred-year-collective trauma from which we have yet to fully recover. And, like the children of Israel, we have sojourned through a philosophical wilderness as Black thinking has developed. The big question we face is, Has God been guiding us toward a promised land?

Dr. Martin Luther King, Jr., in his Memphis speech the night before he died, prophetically answered that question:

We've got some difficult days ahead. But it really doesn't matter with me now. Because I've been to the mountaintop. I won't mind.

Like anybody, I would like to live a long life. Longevity has its place. But I'm not concerned about that now. I just want to do God's will.

And He's allowed me to go up to the mountain. And I've looked over, and I've seen the promised land.

I may not get there with you, but I want you to know tonight that we as a people will get to the promised land.

So I'm happy tonight. I'm not worried about anything. I'm not fearing any man. Mine eyes have seen the glory of the coming of the Lord.[1]

But questions still remain. What is this promised land like? Who is going to lead us there? How can we get there from here?

During the 1960s Black people were really going somewhere. But from the perspective of the '80s, it seems we have been wandering in circles like the children of Israel after they refused to possess the land God had given them (Num 13—14). God had sent ten plagues to break the back of Pharaoh and discredit his pagan gods. He had dealt the mighty Egyptian army, with its superior technology, a major military setback at the Red Sea. He had fed the people from the sky. He had provided fresh water from a pool of poison. They reached the Promised Land one year after leaving Egypt, yet the Israelites failed to believe that the same God who had done all this could defeat some fifth-rate Canaanite tribes.

What was so bizarre was that having decided not to take God and his Word seriously, they wanted to return to Egypt—to slavery and oppression! They wanted to re-adopt those false values which had obliterated their culture and sense of worth.

Where Have All the Leaders Gone?
Today Black America is in a similar situation. We have seen the legal and political victories of the '60s. But now we are in a state of philosophical confusion and cultural disarray. We have a crisis of leadership, of identity. We have slipped into me-ism. Where did this crisis begin?

Much of the generation of leadership which carried us through the '60s has either died naturally, been assassinated or gone off into relative obscurity. King is gone. So is Malcolm. Eldridge Cleaver, Huey Newton, Charles Evers, Stokely Carmichael, Floyd McKissick no longer lead our people. We will not come into our own until a new generation inherits the mantle of leadership. But where will this new Black leadership come from? How will it build on the previous contributions?

Where Our Discussion Will Take Us
These are among the questions we will examine here. In Part I we will briefly look at a variety of concepts and issues which will be discussed more fully in the rest of the book. I want to lay some groundwork for a fresh analysis of some of the great issues in the Black experience. In Part II we will touch on the major phases of Black cultural history and bring out some lessons that we have learned. In Part III we will look at the root of culture as the human

response to God's revelation. We will also look at the crippling effects of humanity's negative response to God on consciousness in general and on Black consciousness in particular. In addition, we will discuss the nature of theology, along with some new ways it can empower our people to reach our cultural potential. Finally, Part IV ties together what we have learned, suggesting how we can apply this knowledge toward developing a new Black agenda.

Though it is written from a Black perspective, this work is not intended to be only a Black book. I have attempted to bring a fresh understanding of how God by his grace is active in culture, using the Black cultural experience as our point of contact. At the back is a glossary of terms that either are used in a specialized sense or cannot be found in a standard dictionary.

It is my prayer that you will be encouraged to know God in new and deeper ways as you gain a new understanding of Afro-American history and culture. Whatever your background may be, I pray that this study will help give you new insights to analyze the culture in which you live. Finally, it is my prayer that the principles contained in this book will play a role in building bridges of understanding and in facilitating reconciliation where there has been alienation.

Part I

A Primer

Chapter 2

Picking Up
the Pieces

I̱T USED TO BE SAID that Western historians had sold us a bill of goods, that what was palmed off as "objective" history was in reality "White" history. Black history was almost completely glossed over as if we did not exist. The same could have been said about the other people-oriented disciplines, such as sociology, psychology and anthropology. This White bias was unseen by White society until the militant brothers of the '60s pointed it out. These new Black thinkers showed us that when people grow up in a particular cultural context, they fail to see the cultural biases they have inherited. They think of their own value system as neutral, the standard for all people. But the leaders of the '60s showed us the folly in this. They pointed out that the White American system of values proclaimed that Black was not beautiful, that the system perpetuated the daily degradation of Black people. The system was not neutral when it came to us.

The Great Rejection

The Black militants rejected American culture and its bias toward everything White. Along with White American culture they rejected Christianity. To them Christianity was the "White man's religion," and the biblical world view was a White world view. The militants in the 1960s looked at the past and found a well-documented case against "Christianity" in its historically poor treatment of our people. Even Black theology as expressed through the oral tradition of the Black church did not escape being tagged as an expression of the White man's religion.

Frederick Douglass, the abolitionist, had also rejected "Christianity," but with one important difference.

Between the Christianity of this land, and the Christianity of Christ, *I recognize the widest possible difference*—so wide, that to receive the one as good, pure, and holy, is of necessity to reject the other as bad, corrupt, and wicked. To be the friend of the one, is of necessity to be the enemy of the other. I love the pure, peaceable, and impartial Christianity of Christ: I therefore hate the corrupt, slaveholding, women-whipping, cradle-plundering, partial and hypocritical Christianity of this land. Indeed, I can see no reason, but the most deceitful one, for calling the religion of this land Christianity. I look upon it as the climax of all misnomers, the boldest of all frauds, and the grossest of all libels.[1]

Unfortunately, the new militants did not do the homework done by one of their patron saints. They were thus unable to distinguish between the "Christianity of Christ" and the "Christianity of this land." The latter I call *White Christianity-ism.**

---

*Christianity-ism: This admittedly ugly and awkward term is the best one, because of its ugliness, to refer to negative religious practices (including racist ones) expressed in the language of Christianity. Christianity-ism strips institutional Christianity of its theological content—God's solution to the problem of human unrighteousness—and leaves only the institution itself which is treated as the object of faith.

When Christianity was rejected, secularism and humanism filled the void. *Secularism* is the belief that human life is independent of God and his revelation and that the sociopolitical struggles of a people transcend all forms of religion. *Humanism* is the belief that humans are the final judge of all truth.[2] Ironically, both of these are world views, with their own belief system and demands for faith. Since this is the essence of religion, secularism and humanism do not transcend religion. They *are* religions themselves. Not realizing this, the secular militants ended up merely switching from a God-centered religion to a man-centered one. They were justified in rejecting White Christianity-ism and asserting that we should replace White definitions of us with definitions of our own. But the militants did not stop there: For them, Black people replaced God himself as the ultimate judges of right and wrong.

A Limited Perspective
Leaving God out had significant results. Not least was that the new Black thinkers lacked an accurate picture of the world because they denied the reality of God.

In 1884 Edwin Abbott published the story of "Flatland." Flatland is an imaginary country where everyone lives in only two dimensions. The people are circles, triangles and squares, and they live in pentagons. A line to them is like a wall to us. They do not know up or down, only north, south, east and west.

One day a sphere came to visit Flatland. At first the Flatlanders could not see him because the sphere remained outside their plane. They were confused by a voice that was not associated with a line, and they did not understand when he told them that he was "above" them (figure 1). So the sphere entered Flatland. Of course, to the Flatlanders he appeared to be a circle. But he talked to them about a three-dimensional world that was beyond their experience (figure 2).

One Flatlander reported that he had been transported temporarily out of Flatland and had experienced three dimensions. Let's call him Squarey. But the people mocked him because they couldn't understand what he was talking about. So Squarey stopped talking. To the Flatlanders whatever was inconceivable in their two-dimensional world must be impossible.[3]

If the Flatlanders had acknowledged that their limited reality was an analogous part of a fuller reality, they could have had a meaningful discussion with the sphere and Squarey about the third dimension. However, because they insisted that Flatland was the ultimate reality, they ended up with a distorted view of reality.

A secular world view is like the Flatlanders' view. Whereas White historians had sold us a bill of goods by leaving Black folks out, Black secularists sold us a bill of goods by leaving God out.

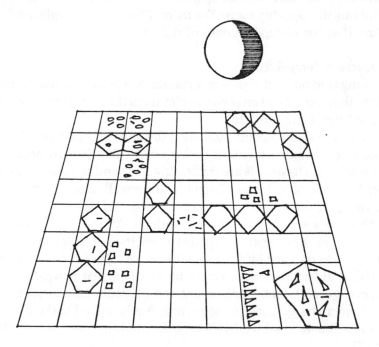

Figure 1: Flatland. Taken from *The Andromedans & Other Parables of Science and Faith* by Denis Osborne © 1977 by Denis Osborne. Used by permission of InterVarsity Press, Downers Grove, Illinois.

Some Black militants insisted that their reality was the ultimate reality. They did not see their reality as analogous to God's reality. God was not even a part of the world as they pictured it. They should have rejected Christianity-ism, but they had no reason for rejecting the one true God. Their perspective was limited, yet they presented this limited perspective as the whole truth. By so doing, they distorted truth.

To a certain extent this limited viewpoint was propagated in the interest of religious neutrality. The secular humanists thought that people could talk about history, math, science, civil rights and so on while ignoring the reality of God. Thus, decisions about moral-

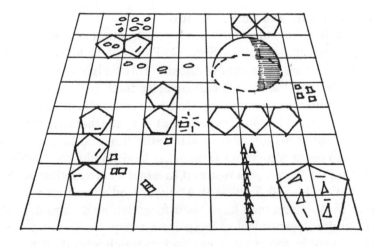

Figure 2: Flatland Invaded. Taken from *The Andromedans and other Parables of Science and Faith* by Denis Osborne © 1977 by Denis Osborne. Used by permission of InterVarsity Press, Downers Grove, Illinois.

ity were left strictly to the individual.

This is what tripped up Eve in the garden of Eden (Gen 3:1-6). She and Adam both knew what good and evil were on the basis of God's Word (Gen 2:16-17). But Satan tempted Eve to take a neutral stance toward God's Word. Satan appealed to Eve as if she were independent of God: "Hey, mama, God says one thing; I say another. Eve, you make the final determination of what is right and wrong."

Eve was not really being neutral. She was rejecting God's word as her basis of judgment. She was attempting to replace God as the ultimate judge. Eve in essence became the first secular humanist.

Likewise, one of the major reasons God turned Israel back from the Promised Land and told them that they would have to wander in the wilderness for forty years was their lack of faith in God. They balked at the border through lack of faith. According to their distorted perspective, the Canaanites were so big they made the Israelites look like grasshoppers.

History, Destiny and Consciousness
What the Israelites needed was a *reconstruction* of their culture. They needed to see things from God's point of view. But only Joshua and Caleb seem to have showed this insight (Num 14:6-9), and they became the new generation of leadership. During the forty years of wilderness wandering, God restructured Israelite culture on the basis of the law and the covenant. He gave them a new way of looking at their history, their present situation and their destiny.

We can learn something from what God taught the Israelites. *First,* God through Moses restored to Israel a correct view of their history (Gen 12—50; Ex 1—18). Many of God's dealings with the family of Abraham may have been forgotten or distorted by the four-hundred-year ordeal of Egyptian slavery.

Black people, too, need to get back in touch with their history. But how? What is the meaning of Black history?

History is never an account of *all* the events of the past. It is instead an account of events which have been sifted and evaluated to determine their significance. History might be called a collection of significant events. But what makes an event significant? To some extent an event is significant if it changed the course of history. So history is a record of events which changed the course of history! How can we understand what is and what is not significant in our past? It will certainly help if we have a God-centered view of the world. If we leave out God, we will have a distorted view, like the folks in Flatland. We need to reflect back on the Word of God if we want to have an adequate understanding of our own past.

Second, God through Moses restored to Israel a correct view of destiny. After four hundred years in slavery and a few months' wandering in the wilderness, the people had forgotten where they were going. God had to remind his people of his specially chosen direction for their lives.

What is the destiny of Black people in America? Where are we going? I believe that we will never know until we return to our roots, to the authentic aspects of Black culture, which includes the Black church. Our destiny will be found there and as we reflect back on the Word of God. God is the Lord of destiny. If we leave God out, we lose our sense of direction.

History and destiny for us are like the third dimension for the Flatlanders. God is not limited by the flow of history, just as the sphere was not limited by the Flatlanders' plane of existence. If Flatland were warped or curved, the Flatlanders would be unconscious of it. They are limited by being *within* their world. The only way to know the contour of Flatland is from the sphere's perspective (figure 3).

Because of our limitations we have no way of knowing the contour of history. We are incapable of knowing to what our destiny points. Since God from his perspective knows all things, he alone is able to guide us through the flow of history toward our true destiny. The Word of God must be our guide to history and destiny. The Word corrects our understanding of reality and completes our picture of the world.

Finally, God through Moses restored to Israel what they needed

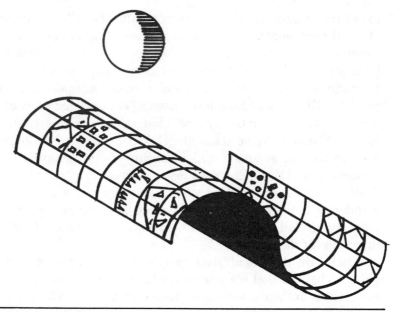

Figure 3: Warped Reality.

for a renewed collective consciousness. What is a collective consciousness? It consists of the standards adopted by a people. An essential aspect in the life of a people, it determines what people do and how they do it in every area of life. The collective consciousness is the grid a people uses to understand their world. It gives rise to their sociology, psychology, anthropology and so on. It is also the key to a people's sense of history and destiny.

How can Black consciousness be defined? What should we as a people recognize as our standards, our values? Only by seeing ourselves as God sees us will we be able to avoid false, self-destructive values. Our values must come from the Word of the one true God.

Culture embodies the cumulative effect of history, destiny and consciousness on the life of a people. Although some have defined culture as "the patterned way in which people do things,"[4] these visible actions are more the manifestation of culture than culture itself (figure 4). Culture itself is made up of commitments, values

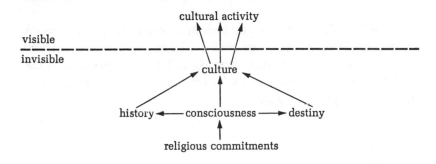

Figure 4: The Relation between Cultural Activity and a People's Values.

and beliefs about the world and people. If the underlying basic commitment is that we are not involved in God's world, then the entire culture will end up with a distorted view of reality. Godlessness will affect every area of life, and this godlessness would be a kind of cultural death.

Yet by Grace

It is unfortunate that the militant Black thinkers attempted to reconstruct Black culture on a commitment to a so-called religiously neutral, secular world view. Because of this the militant movement which developed in the '60s has largely fallen apart. Much Black consciousness has degenerated into do-your-own-thing-ism. Much Black history has been forgotten. Many of our young people barely know what Martin Luther King, Jr., and Malcolm X did.

The militants rejected the scriptural world view without really examining it. They failed to see that Scripture did not come to us from a European or White American context. As a result these leaders made the mistake of leaving God out. Yet by God's grace they were able to make some valuable contributions to us as a people. However, because of the onslaught of do-your-own-thing-ism, we no longer have a cultural framework to tie these contributions together.

In order to pick up the pieces and reconstruct Black culture, we will have to reflect back on what God has revealed about himself and about us. This must be the task of a new generation of Black leadership. Such an arduous task will require the wisdom and understanding available only from God. For the reverence of the Lord, that is the beginning of wisdom; and to depart from evil is understanding (Job 28:28).

Chapter 3

"Oh, Freedom!"

W HEN PEOPLE LACK a basic commitment to God, unrighteousness follows. Scripture describes two types of unrighteousness: ungodliness and oppression. *Ungodliness* happens when people rebel against God and his revelation. Disregarding their responsibility toward God and others, they themselves suffer the consequences of their wrongdoing. *Oppression* occurs when people impose their ungodliness on others, causing them to suffer the consequences. For example, if a person has a racist attitude, he or she is guilty of ungodliness. If, however, that person imposes his racism on others, forcing them to live in substandard conditions, then he is guilty of oppression.

Unrighteousness is never exclusively one or the other; it is always a combination of both. But, we consider oppressors to be people whose unrighteousness is primarily, but not exclusively, oppression. The unrighteousness of oppressed people is primarily, but not exclusively, ungodliness.

Grace as a Base

Unrighteousness is destructive. It destroys humanity. It is only by the grace of God that our humanity has not been so totally destroyed that we are no longer able to resist unrighteousness. If that occurred, the oppressed would be unable to resist oppression. How does resistance relate to righteousness, oppression and our need for God's salvation and grace? I want to look at this next.

1. *Resistance and the righteousness of God.* Theologian James Cone has affirmed that God is on the side of the oppressed.[1] What does this mean? It means that the oppressed, when they resist oppression, are resisting unrighteousness. It does not mean that the oppressed are more righteous than the oppressors, but it does mean they have the opportunity to demonstrate more righteousness. Why? Because resisting oppression is more righteous than giving in to it or inflicting it on others, especially if the oppressed resist righteously. This we will discuss in chapter fourteen. God is the God of righteousness, and in resisting oppression the oppressed align themselves with God. They advance God's justice.

2. *Resistance and the ungodliness of the oppressed.* If ungodliness is imposed on people where their own ungodliness has already diminished their humanity, then the imposed ungodliness is in harmony with their own ungodliness. Consider the prostitute: If she "turns a trick," she cannot charge her "john" with rape. Though her sexuality has been abused, it is her willful intention to be a prostitute. Her intentions complement the intentions of her "john." Nevertheless, just because her intentions match those of her oppressor, this does not mean that she has simply gotten "what she asked for" or that the oppressor ought not to be judged for his oppression. She became a prostitute in the first place partly be-

cause her sense of humanity had been brutalized by oppression and mistreatment.

There is never perfect harmony between oppression and the ungodliness of the oppressed. God set a limit to this unrighteous harmony when he put hostility between Satan, the ultimate oppressor, and humans after the Fall (Gen 3:15). By so doing, God has ensured that for every oppression there will be a corresponding resistance.

3. *Resistance and the oppressed's need for salvation.* If the oppressed focus on their humanity (which oppression is trying to destroy) and try to defend that humanity, then they will be acting righteously. Their own ungodliness will be driven beneath the surface. When liberation comes, however, their ungodliness will resurface with all its negative effects. The oppressed *must* fight to break the back of oppression so they can seek God's solution to their own unrighteousness.

Israel learned this lesson under the judges. They disobeyed God in the first place by not driving out the Canaanites (Deut 7:1-6; Judg 1:27—2:2). The Canaanites regrouped and regained their strength, and they came back to oppress the Israelites. Israel resisted. They cried out to God for help, sought God's ways and were delivered from oppression. But each time they were liberated, their ungodliness resurfaced and they betrayed their call to be a light to the nations. They had to face their own need for salvation.

4. *Resistance and the grace of God.* It is God who has preserved our humanity against total destruction by unrighteousness. He has not let ungodliness and oppression whittle down to nothing his image in people. God cares about justice and has compassionate love for suffering people (Is 58:3-12; Amos 5:10-15, 21-24). God's compassion is rooted in his grace. It is because of God's grace that oppression will ultimately cave in to the resistance of the oppressed.

Thus it is God's grace alone which provides the *basis* for resisting oppression. It is his grace which provides the *power* to resist oppression. It is God's grace which provides the *will* to resist oppression. If we leave God out, we leave out the very possibility of liberation.

A Black Quest

A central theme in the flow of Black history has been the quest for freedom and dignity. There is only one basis for human dignity: the scriptural teaching that man and woman were created in the image of God (Gen 1:26-27). God's personal dignity is the *original* personal dignity. Our dignity is *derived* from the dignity of God. In other words, if God is somebody, which he is, then I am somebody because I in some ways resemble God.

But what is the nature of freedom? Some would say that freedom equals independence. Independence from the oppression of other people is a valid goal, but to attempt independence from God is utterly futile. What makes an airplane fly? Does a wing produce lift because it becomes independent of gravity? Of course not. The wing produces lift precisely *because* of gravity. A wing's lift is an expression of the law of gravity.[2] Trying to be independent of gravity would be as foolish as stepping off the top of a building trying to walk on air. One may think he has succeeded for a few fleeting seconds, but his illusion will end abruptly when he reaches the pavement below.

God laughs at the plots of the nations to rid themselves of his sovereignty because God knows that they simply cannot escape his lordship (Ps 2). "In him we live and move and have our being" (Acts 17:28).

Perhaps we can best learn what his lordship means by determining what it does not mean. We are not robots. His sovereignty does not mean manipulation. Manipulation is our human way of controlling things. For example, as I write sitting at my dining table, I can turn the television set on or off using a remote control. I can make the TV do exactly what I want; that is, I can manipulate the TV. Because we tend to see God as having our limitations, we may imagine that God's sovereignty means that he manipulates us the same way I manipulate the TV. But this is not the case.

There are aspects of the creation which God controls through manipulation. I'm thinking here of the physical and biological laws which determine the behavior of the inanimate world, plants and lower animals. But that is not the way he chooses to control us. He exercises lordship over us through freedom. Human freedom is *derived from* God's lordship and not independent of it, for by definition nothing can be outside God's sovereignty. As Jesus says, "If the Son sets you free, you will be free indeed" (Jn 8:36).

Our difficulty in understanding freedom as a function of God's sovereignty is like the difficulty the Flatlanders had in understanding the third dimension. That it is hard for us to understand "freedom control" does not mean that it is not true. To rebel against God's lordship is to rebel against our own human freedom. If we leave the freedom function of God's lordship, we find ourselves under the manipulation function. To be under manipulation is to be under the slavery of sin (Gal 5:1; Rom 6:16); they are our only two options.

When Adam sinned, for example, he was not exercising free choice; he was rebelling against freedom of choice. "You are free to eat from any tree in the garden" (Gen 2:16). This was the range of freedom. "But you must not eat from the tree of the knowledge [determination] of good and evil, for when you eat of it you will surely die" (Gen 2:17). They were not free to choose to eat the fruit of the forbidden tree so long as they lived under the freedom function of God's sovereignty. Death in this context was not the result of a free choice. On the contrary, it required a willful *rejection* of freedom in order to partake of this fruit and die.

If the Black cultural quest for freedom has been a quest for God's lordship, then Martin Luther King's parting words to us will be fulfilled. We will cross the river Jordan into God's rest—a rest with worldwide implications. But if the Black cultural quest for freedom has been a quest for *independence* from God, then we will end up on the junk heap of the nations—a junk heap of slavery far worse than what we have ever experienced.

Oh, Freedom,
Oh, Freedom,
Oh, Freedom over me!
And before I'll be a slave

I'll be buried in my grave
And go home to my Lord and be free.

This old freedom song is a clear indication that our struggle has not historically been a quest for independence from God. On the contrary, it shows that our quest has been rooted in a desire for God's lordship. Here freedom is not seen as something to be "over," as in recent humanistic thinking, but as something to be "over me." Freedom is being under the right authority; it is being home with my Lord and under the freedom function of God's lordship.

The strength and resilience of the Black church are also an indication that our historic struggle has been a quest for God's freedom. Let us not be hasty to jettison the biblical perspectives of our heritage the way the secular militants did. Maybe we should have listened to A'nt Jane a little more closely.

It is time for a new generation of Joshuas to learn from what has gone before us and, while reflecting back on the Word of God, to build the basis of a renewed Black culture—a renewed culture which will give us a new vision. For "where there is no vision, the people perish" (Prov 29:18 KJV).

Part II

Reflecting Back

Chapter 4

Soul Dynamic

W HEN THE PEOPLE OF JUDAH were captured and taken from Canaan to Babylon, they were confused, to say the least. They had in their possession the Scriptures which stated God's promise that the land of Canaan would be theirs forever. Yet here they were, having lost Canaan, once again captives in a foreign land.

Big questions preyed on the minds of the captive people: If God promised the land to us forever, then how did we end up in this Babylonian predicament? What happened to God's covenant promises? How could God let us down?

Someone was inspired by God to deal with these questions. He plunged into this awesome task by getting hold of three books:

The Annals of Solomon, The Annals of the Kings of Israel and *The Annals of the Kings of Judah*. He proceeded to select material out of these scrolls, analyze it and arrange it into a theological framework. As he did this he reflected back on God, who is absolutely faithful and trustworthy to keep all his promises. In his work he demonstrated that it was not God who failed the covenant, but the people who failed. His work became the books of 1 and 2 Kings.[1]

One of the big questions Black America asks is just this: What are we doing here? It cannot be demonstrated that our arrival in chains was a direct result of our failure. On the contrary, it was the slave traders who were more unfaithful to God. However, the example of how 1 and 2 Kings were written can give a clue to help us reconstruct Black history.

As we study our history, we need to select material out of the body of knowledge, analyze it and arrange it into a theological framework. At the same time we must reflect back on the God who has revealed himself in the Scriptures as the true and living God, absolutely faithful, just and trustworthy. We need to evaluate the contributions made by the outstanding people in our history and see what we can learn from the history of our quest for freedom and dignity.

We need to do this work by building on the insights of men like Martin Luther King, Jr., who told us that in God's economy undeserved suffering can be redemptive (in a narrow sense). With this kind of insight we may discover some new things about freedom and dignity, some new dimensions of truth in Scripture. A dynamic theology will emerge with the understanding of the meaning of Black history as we both study it and reflect back on the Scriptures. With this theology we will be able to weep with righteous anger as we see how our people have suffered, knowing all the time that the suffering has not been in vain.

It is a disgrace that we have not learned to preach "the full counsel of God" through Black history the way Stephen and later Paul were able to preach through Jewish history (Acts 7:2-53; 13:16-41). We talk today about getting back to our roots. But have we shown our roots to be in God? It is a disgrace that we have not taken Black history seriously. It is also a disgrace that we have not learned to disciple the Black community through cultural phenomena besides history.

We must begin somewhere to accomplish this neglected task. Why not here? To begin our task, let's take a look at a few aspects of church history from an African perspective.

The Gospel in Africa

Africa was no stranger to the gospel in the early days of the church. Nor was the African a stranger to the biblical writers.

> Africans were not unknown . . . to the writers of the Bible. Their peculiarities of complexion and hair were as well known to the ancient Greeks and Hebrews as they are to the American people today. And when they spoke of the Ethiopians, they meant the ancestors of the black-skinned and wooly-haired people who . . . have been known as labourers on the plantations of the South. It is to these people, and to their country, that the Psalmist refers, when he says, "Ethiopia shall soon stretch out her hands unto God."[2]

As Jesus was carrying his cross through the streets of Jerusalem, he stumbled under its weight. Simon, a Black man from Cyrene, Africa, was grabbed to carry the cross the rest of the way (Lk 23:26). On the day of Pentecost, people from every nation (including African nations) heard the gospel and were converted (Acts 2:5-12). The Ethiopian government official was converted on his way home (Acts 8:26-39). The church at Antioch had several African members, among them two prophets or teachers, Simeon called the Black man, and Lucius the Cyrenian (Acts 13:1). What were those two Africans doing in Antioch? We find in Acts 11:19-21 that they went there when they found that the non-Jews were not hearing the good news from the Jewish missionaries; the young African church may have been sending missionaries like Simeon and Lucius to plant churches. It is out of that Antioch church that Paul and Barnabas were sent to evangelize Turkey, Greece and

Italy. The European church partly has the African church to thank
for its missionary faithfulness.

Great early scholars like Augustine, Tertullian and Origen were
Black men from Africa.[3] Augustine was a major influence on John
Calvin. So the Reformation theologians have the African church to
thank for a great deal of their theology. There were over five hundred bishops in the African church at one time. In the third century
the Coptic church was formed; however, by the sixth century it had
become spiritually dead. The Muslim conquest finally wiped out
much of the church in North Africa.

In those days the Sahara desert was not so extensive as it is today.
Because of the well-traveled trade routes which crisscrossed Africa
from east to west, the gospel could have penetrated deep into the
interior of Africa. Even now an unbroken line of communication
links the West Coast of Africa, through the Sudan and the so-called
Great Desert, to Asia.

Africa is no vast island, separated by an immense ocean from
other portions of the globe and cut off through the ages from the
men who have made and influenced the destinies of mankind.
Africa has been closely connected, both as source and nourisher,
with some of the most potent influences which have affected for
good the history of the world. The people of Asia and the people
of Africa have been in constant intercourse. No violent social or
political disruption has ever broken through this communication. No chasm caused by war has suspended intercourse.[4]

The foundational truths of the gospel could well have been part of
the basis for the great Mali civilization that arose in West Africa in
the thirteenth century. A Muslim historian described the people
of Mali as "seldom unjust, and [having] a much greater horror
of injustice than any other people. Their sultan shows no mercy
to anyone who is guilty of the least act of it. There is complete
security in their country. Neither traveller nor inhabitant in it has
anything to fear from robbers or men of violence. *It is a real state
whose organization and civilization could be compared with
those of* the Musselman kingdoms, or indeed *the Christian king-*

doms of the same period."⁵

We have a rich African heritage of which we can be proud. We should learn about the great Eastern civilizations such as Ethiopia, Makuria and Alwa, and about the great Western civilizations such as Ghana, Mali and Songhay.⁶ Many of us who have studied our African roots with pride have unfortunately looked at our American experience with shame. Though slavery itself is nothing to rejoice about, the remarkable survival of our people through all the phases of our American experience should be a great encouragement; in it can be seen God's active grace. American slavery was the beginning of racism in our experience. But by grace we resisted these oppressions as we sought for freedom and dignity.

Progress of Consciousness
The historical Black resistance to oppression in the quest for freedom and dignity can be divided into six major phases. Though they were initiated in historical sequence, each still exists today. These phases represent various ways of understanding ourselves and our situation. They are as follows: (1) Colored, (2) Neo-Colored, (3) Negro, (4) Neo-Negro, (5) Black, and (6) Post-Black. The Black phase includes Black awareness, Black power, Black revolutionism, Neo-Black revolutionism and Pan-Africanism. The fulfillment of each or all of these quests will be what I call the Joshua phase.

I have chosen these names for convenience and simplicity, although other names could have served just as well. I do not intend my survey to be exhaustive but to point out some things that God was teaching us through our history.

Each of these pre-Joshua phases has brought us closer to the Jordan, yet none has been able to take us across. Only those whose Black consciousness is reconstructed around the Word of God will be able to implement the Joshua phase. They are the ones who can disciple the Black community through a similar reconstruction of Black culture. At the end of any of these phases the Joshua phase could have emerged, but it didn't happen. And if the discipler of the Black culture today does not seize the present opportunity to implement a Joshua-phase reconstruction, then we will continue to wander in philosophical circles.

Before we examine the actual phases of our history, let's review the context out of which grew the early forms of Black consciousness.

Slave Resistance
Columbus Salley and Ronald Behm write about the experience of slavery:

> The series of traumatic shocks involved had such an effect upon the Africans that their personality development was altered to suit the image and likeness of a system that assumed their inferiority.

> First, there was the shock of being captured. "The second shock—the long march to the sea—drew out the nightmare for many weeks. . . . Hardship, thirst, brutalities, and near starvation penetrated the experience of each exhausted man and woman who reached the coast." It was also shocking to be sold to foreign traders, and then branded and herded into a strange ship. Then came the protracted and stupefying Middle Passage from Africa to the Americas. This dread transportation involved severe overcrowding, frequent rape, fatal disease and cruel beatings, all of which served to establish a master's absolute domination. The final shock came with a seasoning period in the West Indies during which slaves were taught obedience and cringing submission to their masters. . . .

> As an African came to America he was easily "fitted" for his work because he was divorced from his native culture and language. His number was inexhaustible, and his physical characteristics made identification unmistakable. As rationale and justification for the system, he was reputed (falsely) to come from an uncivilized world, thus making slavery the means to the graces of white, Western . . . civilization.[7]

The whole basis of this dehumanizing practice was an illegitimate view of Black humanity—a view in which skin color determined not only a person's status but the presence or lack of the image of God. It became a time-honored belief among many adherents of White Christianity-ism that this uprooted African had no soul. Black people were therefore classified as nonhuman—in later history as three-fifths human. So raping a female slave was not a crime, nor was it considered fornication or adultery.

Yet something positive began to develop in the consciousness of the enslaved Africans, something so significant that it would have a profound effect on Black culture from the days of slavery up to the present. The slaves learned about God.

The early masters, with few exceptions, had never intended that slaves should become Christian. However, this did not prevent the slaves from experiencing the power of the Word of God. As I pointed out in chapter three, resistance to oppression is itself an expression of the grace of God.

When a people are subjected to such oppression, they are driven inward to the depths of the very humanity the oppression is trying to negate. Any cultural expressions which emerge from such a suffering people will come from those human depths. Other human beings who encounter these expressions will be affected at comparable depths. This, I believe, is what LeRoi Jones meant when he described us as the "Blues People."[8] This cultural depth and the skills to express such depth are what is today popularly known as "soul."

One reason soul culture is so penetrating is that humanity is in the image of God, and through it God reveals his personhood and power. The deeper we go into our humanity, the more we experience God's power. This is part of the reason the existence of God was never a matter of argument in historic Black thinking. Black culture always presupposed God. Soul culture thus became fertile ground for the reception of the gospel.

On Sunday mornings those slaves who drove their masters to church began to hear interesting things as they stood at the windows. They began to set their fellow slaves on fire as they shared what they had heard. They began to get the notion that they were created in the image of God, that they had human worth and that being a slave was a contradiction to their dignity as human beings.

Black spirituals like "Swing Low, Sweet Chariot," and "Free at Last" became examples of historic Black theology, and the writings and sayings of Frederick Douglass expressed the practical outworking of Black theology. Frederick Douglass, Harriet Tubman and many other Black exponents of freedom were Christians. The underground railroad itself became an application of the "good news."

As the fires of revival began to spread among some of the slaves, freedom from slavery came to symbolize human dignity, the outworking of salvation in this life. This, of course, presented a problem:

> Christianity was a major barrier to be hurdled on the way to chattel racial slavery. There was an unwritten law that a Christian could not be held as a slave. Therefore, if Blacks were allowed to be converted, they could no longer be slaves, and baptism would be tantamount to emancipation. . . . To settle any doubt, the leading colony of Virginia in "a series of laws between 1667 and 1671 laid down the rule that conversion alone did not lead to a release from servitude." Finally, the Church of England accepted the position stated by Morgan Godwyn in 1680 that "Christianity" and slavery were *fully compatible.*[9]

This fully compatible "Christianity" was in reality slavemaster Christianity-ism, which the Black militants in the 1960s identified as the White man's religion. Since the slavemasters' attempt to stamp out or suppress the slave revival proved to be futile, they tried instead to pre-empt it. They attempted to force on the slaves their own "more appropriate" Christianity-ism.

> With the problem of the status of Christian slaves settled, efforts were made to spread ["Christianity"] among Blacks. In 1701 the Society for the Propagation of the Gospel in Foreign Parts (S.P.G.) was organized as a missionary arm of the Anglican Church. Its missionaries who worked among the slaves were opposed by slavemasters who were reluctant to allow time to their slaves

for religious instruction. . . .

Those who were influenced were taught doctrine designed to support slavery, almost to the exclusion of the historic dogmas of the Christian faith. So, very early in colonial life an intimate and inseparable union between "Christianity" and the institution of slavery was effected.[10]
The Scriptures themselves warn us that "the time will come when men will not put up with sound doctrine" (2 Tim 4:3). Slavery had opened the door for the emergence of unchristian Christianity-ism. But 2 Timothy goes on to say, "Instead, to suit their own desires, . . . they will turn their ears away from the truth and turn aside to myths" (vv. 3-4). Such myths became the basic ingredients of slave-master Christianity-ism. Let's look at some of these myths.

A Mark, a Curse and a Spook
First, a myth was created about the *"mark of Cain."* According to Genesis 4:1-15 Cain, a farmer, rebelled against God and killed his brother Abel, a shepherd. As a result God punished Cain by putting the ground under a curse. Nothing would grow for him. Cain was condemned to be a homeless wanderer for the rest of his life.

Cain appealed to God on the grounds that (1) the punishment was too hard for him to bear, and (2) he was afraid he'd be killed by anyone who found him. As an act of grace God put a mark on Cain as a warning to everyone not to kill him. God told Cain that if anyone killed him, God would take *seven* lives in revenge.

The myth declared that the mark on Cain was dark skin. But the Bible neither says nor implies that this mark had anything to do with skin color. The Scripture just says that the mark was a warning not to kill Cain. (If the mark of Cain were dark skin, as some have dogmatically believed, then woe to those who have hurt or killed dark-skinned people, for they will be avenged by God sevenfold!) Of course, we will never know what the mark of Cain really was, since all of Cain's descendants were killed in the flood.

A second myth revolved around *a curse on Ham and his descendants.* This myth is rooted in a twisted interpretation of Genesis

9:18-28. According to the passage, Noah had three sons: Shem, Ham and Japheth. (Ham was the father of Canaan.) Noah planted a vineyard, made some wine, drank too much, got drunk, took off his clothes and lay naked in his tent. Ham discovered his father in his drunken, naked state; he told his brothers to take care of their father, and they did.

This was no sin on Ham's part. However, according to the myth, Ham laughed at Noah and mocked him. But Scripture neither records nor implies such irreverence on Ham's part.

When Noah sobered up and learned "what his *youngest son* had done to him," he cursed Canaan and his descendants. Advocates of the Ham myth deliberately ignore the fact that Hebrew had no word for grandson. Noah's "youngest son" was really his youngest male descendant. This was Canaan, Ham's youngest son and Noah's youngest grandson. It was *Canaan* and not Ham who irreverently took advantage of Noah's drunken condition and did something horrible to Noah. It was *Canaan* who left Noah naked in his tent.

Thus the curse fell on Canaan and his descendants, the Canaanites, who would follow his perverted example (Gen 19:1-9). All the Canaanite kingdoms were eventually destroyed, fulfilling the curse on Canaan (2 Sam 8; 1 Chron 18:1-13; Ps 135:1-12). One thing is clear. Ham and his other descendants had nothing to do with this curse. Ham was also the father of Cush, Egypt and Lybia (Gen 10:6-14), who are the fathers of the peoples of Africa. This curse has absolutely nothing to do with Africans or Afro-Americans.

The third myth espoused *a totally otherworldly Jesus*. If the slave system were to be preserved, then the slavemasters could not afford for the slaves to have a biblical Jesus who was fully human and fully divine. Such a Jesus might have something to do with salvation in *this* life. The slaves might get some dangerous ideas from Jesus' statements like "The Spirit of the Lord is on me, because he has anointed me . . . to proclaim freedom for the prisoners and . . . to release the oppressed" (Lk 4:18).

The humanity of Christ in particular presented a problem. If

Jesus was really a man of southwest Asian or northeast African descent, then he might look more like the slaves than the slavemasters. Thus an exclusively White Jesus was substituted, a "man" who was totally otherworldly. This Jesus offered a salvation restricted to the hereafter. Jesus' humanity was diminished almost to nothing, and his divinity was made abstract. This fake Jesus was nothing more than a spineless spook and bore little resemblance to the biblical Christ. According to Scripture, Jesus came by way of Incarnation (Jn 1:14); this mythological Jesus, however, was an invention of the spirit of antichrist, according to 1 John 4:1-3.

Soul Force
Slavemaster Christianity-ism was rejected by most Christian slaves, but under its cover they began to develop an indigenous theological outlook and practice. We began using a "double meaning" language which was passed down in our oral tradition. When the master was present in Black worship, he would think the slaves were singing and shouting about one thing (spiritual freedom, perhaps) when in reality they were thinking of another (freedom *this side* of heaven).

Because the Black church has not produced written confessions and creeds, it has often been said that it has not produced a theology. However, we cannot overlook the fact that for many reasons, including the fact that our people were long denied access to reading and writing, we have been an oral and not a literary people. To say that we have no theology because we have not produced it in literature is like saying that the Jews of the exodus had no revelation before Sinai. The Jews were always singing about something, and these songs came to be recorded in the five books of Moses. It is within our oral tradition that we find historic Black theology. The rich oral tradition of the Black church—its music and its preaching—is the locus of theology in Black culture.

The power of soul force was greatly multiplied by the power of God's Word because the only channel of expression allowed Black people was the church. We learned to transform the Bible from its written form into an oral form, using soul culture. We produced a theological dynamic that captured nuggets of biblical truth in forceful phrases and images of life experience; we created a cultural dynamic of deeply moving expressions of Black consciousness reflecting the image of God in us. These two merged to become the soul dynamic which simmered, grew and mellowed through the days of slavery.

For our people, the written Word of God was like powdered milk, having all the nutrients of whole milk yet undrinkable because it was in the wrong form. Transforming the written Word of God into an oral Word of God was like adding water.[11] Though this transformed Word of God does not have the same authoritative weight as Scripture, it made the Word of God "drinkable" and had a powerful effect. Viewed comparatively, this theological dynamic was to classical Christian theology as art is to science; as intuitive knowledge is to cognitive knowledge; as the concrete is to the abstract; as the multidimensional is to the linear; as a mental image is to a concept.[12]

Since the Black struggle has been against ethical wrongdoing, the theology of the Black church has been essentially ethical. Since the major theme which runs throughout Black history is the quest for true freedom and human dignity, the early days of this quest were a struggle to be consistent to God's image despite the forces of dehumanization. Thus, from the days of slavery up to the present moment, the Black experience has been a struggle against personal, institutional and legal wrongs which attempt to negate our humanity, our culture and our constitutional rights. Though we will discuss it more fully in chapter twelve, it would be helpful at this time to take a brief look at this theological dynamic from three perspectives: its content, its context and its experience.

Content. Redemptive history is not treated as information merely to be analyzed and imparted. The events are to be dramatized by the preacher so that the whole congregation can join him in celebrating God's present grace and faithfulness, while reflecting back on God's grace and faithfulness as revealed in the scriptural accounts.

This is the genius of Black preaching. James Cone describes it in *God of the Oppressed:*

> *The form of Black religious thought is expressed in the style of story and its content is liberation.* .... [Black people during slavery] intuitively perceived that the problem of the auction block and slave drivers would not be solved through philosophical debate. The problem had to be handled on the level of concrete history as that history was defined by the presence of the slave-masters. Slaves therefore had to devise a language commensurate with their social situation. That was why they told stories. Through the medium of stories, Black slaves created concrete and vivid pictures of their past and present existence, using the historical images of God's dealings with his people and thus breaking open the future for the oppressed not known to ordinary historical observation.[13]

Context. Black theology emphasizes the event of worship empowered by "the move of the Spirit" and our participation in the event. This is why expressions are chosen not for their rational value, but for their emotive value; not for accuracy but for beauty. Historic Black theology is not a spectator sport. The response of the listener is as much a part of preaching as the proclamation itself: "Can I get a witness?" asks the preacher. Celebration is the very cornerstone of Black worship; it is commonly called "having chu'ch."

Experience. Black theology is experiential and collective. When you listen to Black preaching, you hear "I" a great deal. It would be easy but wrong to conclude that this is individualistic. Rather, in good traditional Black preaching there is an intercourse between the preacher's proclamation and the congregation's response which reaches its climax when the preacher becomes one with the congregation. At this point the preacher becomes prophet for the people. When he says "I," it becomes a collective "I" for the congregation. It is an experience which illustrates the mystical union of Christ and his church.

This dynamic became the heart of the collective expression of

Black resistance to White oppression. It was also the driving force behind the emergence of Black culture. We were a people of different languages and cultures in Africa. Yet when the attempt was made to strip us of all humanity through oppression, the soul dynamic of resistance by God's grace emerged, not only giving us what we need to survive the horrors of slavery, but also galvanizing us into a cultural nation.

We have not always been good stewards of our soul dynamic. Witness our neglect of its ethical implications as hostility existed among various groups based on complexion or status. Witness too our failure on occasion to apply the cultural power of the soul dynamic to resisting oppression. At various times in our history we have misapplied it to "accommodating" oppression instead of overcoming it.

Yet the soul dynamic was there drawing us together as a people. We must remember that no nation has ever been a good steward of the gracious gifts of God. We are all unrighteous. However, in spite of human attempts to cut us off from God and make us nobodies, God made us somebody by bringing forth the Black cultural nation so that by his grace we would "seek him and perhaps reach out for him and find him, though he is not far from each one of us. 'For in him we live and move and have our being' " (Acts 17:27-28).

Chapter 5

A Formative Phase

OUR QUEST FOR FREEDOM and dignity has been shaped by the theological dynamic. Thus when we've been true to it our quest for freedom has been a quest for the freedom of God's lordship. And our quest for dignity has been a quest for the being of God because we have our being, our dignity, in him. When we look at the six phases of Black American history from this perspective, we will see that, though ultimate freedom and dignity eluded us, we learned some valuable lessons about what it means to possess them in this life. Let's now take a closer but brief look at our formative phase and its aftermath.

Colored

The Colored phase of our history was born in slavery. In it the myth of White supremacy was imposed on us along with White standards. "Colored" ("darky" and "nigger" are equivalent terms), a label chosen for us by the slavemasters, allowed for division among our people. "House slaves" were usually the products of the masters' sexual exploitation of the slaves. They were lighter in complexion and enjoyed a better quality of life than other slaves. Consequently they tended to be more devoted to the master than were the other Black brothers and sisters. "Field slaves," the workers and overseers, were usually darker in complexion and shared a contempt for the master.

The sexual exploitation of the slave woman caused a tangled net of trouble for everyone. (1) The Black man suspected the White man of having designs on his woman; (2) the Black man suspected the Black woman because he was never sure that she could be all his, even if she wanted to be; (3) The White woman suspected the Black woman of being the object of her husband's exploitation; and (4) the White man suspected the Black man, fearing that his male slave might do to his White woman what he was doing to the slave woman. The male slavemaster who sexually neglected his wife to exploit Black women was also afraid that his wife might seek satisfaction from the male slave. Portraying the Black male as a "stud" only aggravated his fear. Ironically this White-generated fear was blamed on the Black male. By the time of the Reconstruction it had evolved into a mass paranoia which became the main rationale for the formation of the Ku Klux Klan and which contributed to the roots of postslavery racism.

Suspicion between the house slaves and field slaves, as well as between Black women and Black men, established a pattern of intra-Black mistrust among our people which lasted through many years. This negative self-image tended to keep anger and frustration internalized and served to free the masters from much of their worry of a slave revolt. Though the hearts of most slaves longed for freedom, the brute force of the institution of slavery prevented all but a very few from actualizing it. So the hope of freedom in the Colored phase became tied mostly to the hereafter.

In the early foundations of Black theology, the "second exodus" became a major theme. The river Jordan represented death. On this side of the Jordan we lived in the Egypt of slavery, where we were the least among the American cultures. On the other side of the Jordan we would be free to be with our Lord in the promised land, and we'd be first among the American cultures (figure 5).

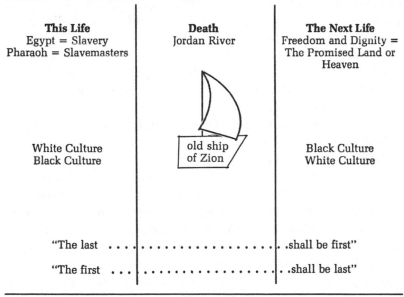

This Life	**Death**	**The Next Life**
Egypt = Slavery	Jordan River	Freedom and Dignity =
Pharaoh = Slavemasters		The Promised Land or
		Heaven
White Culture	old ship	Black Culture
Black Culture	of Zion	White Culture
"The last	. . . .	. .shall be first"
"The first . . .	. . . .	. .shall be last"

Figure 5: Structure of Early Black Theology.

Though we did not achieve true freedom and human dignity at this time, we did learn several things during the Colored phase. Through the pain of exploitation we realized that slavery as practiced could never allow Black people the personal dignity the Bible declares open to all. We saw the parallel between our oppressed condition and that of the ancient Hebrews. Though faith in Christ promised us freedom on the other side of death, we were awakened in faith

also to pursue freedom on *this* side of the Jordan. We learned that
life cannot be lived on an otherworldly basis, with hope only for
the hereafter. In short, we learned that the God of Christianity was
truly God, while the god offered us in Christianity-ism was no god
at all.

Non-Slavery to Neo-Slavery

After the Civil War and the Emancipation Proclamation, the end of
slavery was no longer a dream but reality. The remarkable political
and social progress made by Blacks during Reconstruction gave our
people hope that the scars of slavery would soon be eliminated
from our collective psyche.

An ex-slave, Blanche Kelso Bruce, was representing Mississippi
in the United States Senate. Pinckney Benton Stewart Pinch-
back, young, charming, daring, was sitting in the governor's
mansion in Louisiana.

In Mississippi, in South Carolina, in Louisiana, Negro lieu-
tenant governors were sitting on the right hand of power. A
Negro was secretary of state in Florida; a Negro was on the state
supreme court in South Carolina. Negroes were superintendents
of education, state treasurers, adjutant generals, solicitors,
judges and major generals of militia. Robert H. Wood was mayor
of Natchez, Mississippi, and Norris Wright Cuney was running
for mayor of Galveston, Texas. Seven Negroes were sitting in
the House of Representatives.[1]

However, the "freedom" wrought by the Emancipation Proclamation turned out to fall short of true freedom. It was nullified in the
sudden death of Reconstruction in 1877 at the inauguration of
President Hayes. Hayes for political reasons withdrew from the
South the federal troops which had been enforcing the provisions
of the Fourteenth and Fifteenth Amendments. The former slaves
were thereby abandoned to the devices of those who wanted to re-
establish White supremacy. As a result, a neo-slavery emerged—a
system of oppression rooted in political disenfranchisement, racial
segregation and exploitive economic relationships which subju-

gated Blacks to Whites. This became known as the Jim-Crow backlash.[2]

Roughly contemporary with the Jim-Crow backlash in the South was the industrial revolution of the North. The industrial revolution had a far-reaching impact on the American population. During the last quarter of the nineteenth century a wave of immigrants from Europe had washed over the United States. America was becoming a multiethnic, multicultural and multilingual society, especially in the northeastern cities. In the minds of many, American society had to find a way to stay culturally American. Thus developed the concept of the "melting pot." The public school system became the ideal vehicle for inculcating the melting pot value system.

What the Jim-Crow backlash achieved in the South, the melting pot concept achieved in the North, namely, the exclusion of Black people from mainstream American life. Not everyone could melt into the pot, only the European immigrants. And their ability to melt was directly related to their closeness to Anglo-Saxon culture.[3] This bleak situation was further aggravated because the Jim-Crow movement spilled over into the North and the melting pot movement spilled over into the South.

The White Church in Transition
Many White Christians had been faithful to the cultural mandate of Jesus Christ during Reconstruction. They brought education and other forms of help to the former slaves. When the pressure of Jim-Crowism arose in the late 1870s, however, they were forced to abandon the Black community, leaving us to face the horrors of the southern racist backlash alone.

Another concern was taking the White Christian's attention. Just after the turn of the twentieth century, the battle of the Bible began heating up. On one side were those who followed in the footsteps of others who a century earlier had given in to the basic assumptions of secular humanism. As a result, their Christianity had eroded into an empty Christianity-ism with a god whose substance depended on human definition and human opinion. For them, Jesus was a mere man—a prophet at best—and the Bible was a merely human book containing some passages which might be considered "inspired" in some vague way. These people became known as liberals, or modernists.

The liberals had lost their theological direction and had nothing to do but play connotation word games. This all changed when in 1907 Walter Rauschenbusch published _Christianity and the Social Crisis_.[4] Advocating social action and neglecting personal salvation, this "social gospel" breathed new life into the liberal movement.

On the other side of the battle were those who, reacting against the liberals, advocated personal salvation and orthodox doctrine over social action. They became known as "fundamentalists," or "conservatives." Those who stood for the conceptual authority of Scripture took the fundamentalist side, and those who stood for the ethical authority of Scripture took the liberal side. To make a sharp distinction between themselves and the liberals, many fundamentalists divested themselves of _all_ social involvement and concentrated on merely getting people "saved." They wrongly identified social action with liberalism rather than Christian action. Furthermore, the fiascoes of Prohibition[5] (1920-32) and the Scopes trial[6] (1925) made fundamentalists feel the heat of cultural defeat. This effectively closed the books on fundamentalist cultural involvement and opened the door for secular humanism.

The Bible itself never makes such a dichotomy between personal salvation and social action, between conceptual and ethical authority. So in essence both sides lost the battle of the Bible. Between 1877 and 1930 the White Bible-believing churches developed a double isolation from the Black community. They capitulated to White racism, and they adopted a socially impotent gospel. The rift was deep in that social ethics and the quest for freedom and dignity lay at the heart of historic Black theology. The social retreat of the White church became known as the Great Reversal. White, Bible-believing Christianity had come to resemble White Christianity-ism.

In spite of the abandonment of the White Christians, the Black church had the theological dynamic which had been brewing throughout the days of slavery. By the time of the Emancipation we had seen one of the most powerful examples of the spread of the gospel since the days of Paul. America witnessed a most astonishing success of Protestantism in the overwhelming conversion of the Black community.[7] This explosive growth of the Black church between 1860 and 1910, the harvest of seed planted a century or more earlier, has remained thus far unparalleled in American history.

The Black church was utterly bewildered at the sudden abortion of Reconstruction and the onslaught of the Jim-Crow backlash. By the 1880s and '90s it had yet to apply Black theology to deal with the realities of disenfranchisement. Because they had lost the practice of the old, practical Black theology, Jim-Crow Christianity-ism was imposed on large segments of the Black church in the South. So the Black church became an "accommodative church."[8] "The preachers in these churches oriented their members to White domination in society. As Black ministers had played the role of mediator and spokesman before the Civil War, so they continued during this period. In terms of race relations, the Black churches' main function was to accommodate their members to their subordinate status in White Society."[9]

The attempt to apply the theological dynamic to accommodation temporarily crippled the Black church. But that did not stop the quest for freedom and dignity. It continued, but no longer within the bounds of church culture. The church would later recover from this paralysis and again become a major force in the quest, but the next two phases developed without leadership from the church. In the next chapter we will look at these phases as well as the branches into which the quest divided.

Chapter 6

Two Streams

WITH THE EMERGENCE of post-Reconstruction oppression, the Black resistance moved toward two goals: to overcome the effects of Jim Crow in the South and to enter into the melting pot in the North. The quest would now flow in two streams, northern and southern.

Both streams have attempted to achieve freedom and dignity by two strategies, integration (or desegregation) and consolidation around Black cultural resources. The southern stream first tried a consolidation strategy, the Neo-Colored phase of our history.

Neo-Colored
Booker T. Washington was the main exponent of the Neo-Colored

phase. He told us that we needed to consolidate around the skills and resources we had gained from slavery and earn freedom and dignity. In his 1895 address to a White audience at the Atlanta Exposition, Booker T. said:

A ship lost at sea for many days suddenly sighted a friendly vessel. From the mast of the unfortunate vessel was seen a signal, "Water, water; we die of thirst!" The answer from the friendly vessel at once came back, "Cast down your bucket where you are." A second time the signal, "Water, water; send us water!" ran up from the distressed vessel, and was answered, "Cast down your bucket where you are." And a third and fourth signal for water was answered, "Cast down your bucket where you are." The captain of the distressed vessel, at last heeding the injunction, cast down his bucket, and it came up full of fresh, sparkling water from the mouth of the Amazon river. To those of my race . . . , I would say: "Cast down your bucket where you are"—cast it down in making friends in every manly way of the people of all races by whom we are surrounded.

Cast it down in agriculture, mechanics, in commerce, in domestic service, and in the professions. . . . No race can prosper till it learns that there is as much dignity in tilling a field as in writing a poem. It is at the bottom of life we must begin, and not at the top. . . .

To those of the white race . . . I say . . . you can be sure in the future, as in the past, that you and your families will be surrounded by the most patient, faithful, law-abiding, and unresentful people that the world has seen. As we have proved our loyalty to you in the past, in nursing your children, watching by the sickbed of your mothers and fathers, and often following them with tear-dimmed eyes to their graves, so in the future, in our humble way, we shall stand by you with a devotion that no foreigner can approach, ready to lay down our lives, if need be, in defense of yours, interlacing our industrial, commercial, civil, and religious life with yours in a way that shall make the interests of both races one. In all things that are purely social we can be as separate as the fingers, yet one as the hand in all things essential to mutual progress.[1]

In other words, if we proved ourselves worthy and industrious enough in our humble manual and skilled labor, the White folks would eventually welcome us. This optimism about the good will of White people was the major premise of White humanism among Blacks. It did not bear fruit. White folks refused to accept our hard work. And after the European immigrants learned our skills, which we freely shared with them, we were systematically eliminated from the skilled labor force through White-only trade unions. Hence a major portion of the southern-based Neo-Colored strategy was nullified by racism, and the rest of this phase slowly faded.

Though it did not work for us, the Neo-Colored movement did set a workable pattern for other ethnic groups. And we learned several things for ourselves during this phase. First, mere non-slavery provided neither true freedom nor human dignity. Second, we needed to consolidate around our existing resources as a people. Third, it was essential that we develop the resources we already had if we were going to achieve our goal. White humanism had proved to be a farce as far as we were concerned; White standards gave us no ground for or means of dignity. If we wanted to melt in, we'd have to find another way than the good graces of Whites or the honest labor of our hands.

Around 1900 northern men like W. E. B. DuBois and Monroe Trotter began to fire blistering criticisms at Booker T. Washington. They saw the need to pull together as a cultural nation and deal with our situation from a position of militant educational strength. However, these men proved to be too far ahead of their time. Their ideas did not catch on among the northern Black population of that time. The North had been a haven for Blacks during slavery, and it was harder for them to see the deep problems of life in the North, having seen it so much worse in the South.

Following World War 1 large numbers of Black people migrated from the South to the northern cities in search of jobs and a better way of life. This migration swelled the population, especially in the northeastern cities, and the time came when they would no longer be satisfied with the slight measure of dignity allotted them there.

Negro

As selected European cultures began to melt into the melting pot, the Black cultural nation which lacked European roots began to burn, crushed by the weight of the melting pot against the hot coals of oppression. Freedom and dignity were taken from our grasp as they appeared to be locked inside the melting pot. Entering the pot became the new hope of achieving freedom and dignity.

For some northern Blacks, getting into the melting pot by any means necessary was all that mattered. As a result, in the early '20s a consensus began to well up among those who were seriously trying to enter. This consensus I call the Negro phase. Those involved in this strategy learned some lessons from failure of the Neo-Colored phase. But they never saw the need to consolidate our people, nor did they jettison the baggage of White humanism. They thought that the problem was not White humanism but rather the strategy we employed to make it come alive. They agreed that to achieve melting pot status, one had to become just like the melting pot folks. So the key strategy of the Negro phase became one of imitation.

A certain young man observed this when he lived in Boston during the late 1930s:

> I saw those Roxbury Negroes acting and living differently from any black people I'd ever dreamed of in my life.... What I thought I was seeing ... were high-class, educated, important Negroes, living well, working in big jobs and positions.... These Negroes walked along the sidewalks looking haughty and dignified, on their way to work, to shop, to visit, to church. ... They prided themselves on being incomparably more "cultured," "cultivated," "dignified," and better off than their black brethren down in the ghetto, which was no further away than you could throw a rock. Under the pitiful misapprehension that

it would make them "better," these Hill Negroes were breaking their backs trying to imitate white people.

Any black family that had been around Boston long enough to own the home they lived in was considered among the Hill elite. It didn't make any difference that they had to rent out rooms to make ends meet. Then the native-born New Englanders among them looked down upon recently migrated Southern home-owners who lived next door....

In those days on the Hill, any who could claim "professional" status—teachers, preachers, practical nurses—also considered themselves superior....

I'd guess that eight out of ten of the Hill Negroes of Roxbury, despite the impressive-sounding job titles they affected, actually worked as menials and servants. "He's in banking," or "He's in securities." It sounded as though they were discussing a Rockefeller or a Mellon—and not some grayheaded, dignity-posturing bank janitor, or bond-house messenger. "I'm with an old family" was the euphemism used to dignify the professions of white folks' cooks and maids who talked so affectedly among their own kind in Roxbury that you couldn't even understand them. I don't know how many forty- and fifty-year-old errand boys went down the Hill dressed like ambassadors in black suits and white collars, to downtown jobs "in government," "in finance," or "in law." It has never ceased to amaze me how so many Negroes, then and now, could stand the indignity of that kind of self-delusion.[2]

Hence some of us began to "talk proper," desire a pale complexion, avoid getting sun tans, and straighten our hair. The same young observer also described what he went through in his pre-Black days to get a hairstyle (a "conk") that looked like straight White hair.

The congolene [a mixture of eggs, potatoes and lye] just felt warm when Shorty [his best friend] started combing it in. But then my head caught fire.

I gritted my teeth and tried to pull the sides of the kitchen table together. The comb felt as if it was raking my skin off.

My eyes watered, my nose was running. I couldn't stand it any longer; I bolted to the washbasin. I was cursing Shorty with every name I could think of when he got the spray going and started soap-lathering my head.

He lathered and spray-rinsed, lathered and spray-rinsed, maybe ten or twelve times, each time gradually closing the hot-water faucet, until the rinse was cold, and that helped some.

"You feel any stinging spots?"

"No," I managed to say. My knees were trembling.

"Sit back down, then. I think we got it all out okay."

The flame came back as Shorty, with a thick towel, started drying my head, rubbing hard. *"Easy, man, easy!"* I kept shouting.

"The first time's always worst. You get used to it better before long. You took it real good, homeboy. You got a good conk."

When Shorty let me stand up and see in the mirror, my hair hung down in limp, damp strings. My scalp still flamed, but not as badly; I would bear it. He draped the towel around my shoulders . . . and began again vaselining my hair.

I could feel him combing, straight back, first the big comb, then the fine-toothed one. . . .

My first view in the mirror blotted out the hurting. I'd seen some pretty conks, but when it's the first time, on your own head, the transformation, after the lifetime of kinks, is staggering. . . .

On top of my head was this thick, smooth sheen of shining red hair—real red—as straight as any white man's. . . .

How ridiculous I was! Stupid enough to stand there simply lost in admiration of my hair now looking "white."

This was my first really big step toward self-degradation: when I endured all of that pain, literally burning my flesh to have it look like a white man's hair. I had joined that multitude of Negro men and women in America who are brainwashed into believing that the black people are "inferior"—and white people "superior"—that they will even violate and mutilate their God-created bodies to try to look "pretty" by white standards.[3]

Because *Negro* was a label chosen for us by Whites, it allowed for gradation in color. We even learned to discriminate against ourselves on the basis of color. If a Negro happened to have a very pale complexion, naturally straight hair and a mastery of "proper talk," he was able to "pass for White" and melt into the pot. Some estimate that we lost at least fifty thousand Negroes a year this way.

The Negro strategy of the urban North had bought a pseudo-sophisticated lifestyle. And the religious expression of this movement I call "Polly Parrot Christianity-ism." It was a form of the old "White man's religion" minus the supernatural; in it God was unimportant. An ultracold style of worship replaced the practices of historic Black theology. Heaven and hell were considered myths, and jumping, shouting, rhythm and other expressions of emotion were considered uncivilized. They were ashamed of the soul dynamic and tried to distance themselves from it.

But how could people be free if they were not free to be themselves? How could people find dignity if they were ashamed of their cultural ethnic heritage? To pretend to be White is bondage to a lie and demeaning to a person's character. After all, what would the Negro who was "passing" do if his White associates found out that he was not White?

Though we did not achieve freedom and dignity, we learned several things through the Negro phase. We learned that the strategy of imitation is unworkable for most of our people because it is based on factors of genetics and environment over which we have no control. And we learned that imitating the melting pot lifestyle, racism and standards leads to intra-Negro complexion consciousness, self-hatred, feelings of inferiority and economic stress. Though it did not work for us, the Negro movement set a pattern for other ethnic groups that did prove successful for them.

Along with urbanization also came ghettoization which victimized those who did not have the imitational skills, physical characteristics, money or willingness to practice "Negro" lifestyle. Housing discrimination killed any chance for a Black person to escape the ghetto the way some other ethnic groups were doing.

Obviously these folks did not practice Polly Parrot Christianity-ism, and from them emerged a new type of Black church which was in some ways the forerunner of the Neo-Negro church (see chapter seven). "The Black church, which had given Black people a sur-vival style in a hostile White world, responded to urbanization and White withdrawal by developing a new mental outlook concerning its role in American society. The increasing economic diversity of the Black community in the city transformed the accommodative Black church" into a political church.[4]

As it began to recover from the crippling effects of being squeezed into the role of accommodation, this new urban church began to take a more active role in the life of the Black community.

As large middle-class and mixed-class congregations grew up in the urban center, the preacher was expected to devote more time to community affairs and the advancement of the race. These activities, as always, were within the accepted limitations of the White power structure. They therefore consisted largely of im-provements in housing, education and the like rather than in "social equality and integration with whites."

Even within this change of perspective by Black churches, traditional loyalty to the Baptist and Methodist churches pre-vailed. But the predominantly otherworldly outlook and con-cern for the purely "spiritual" was diminished. A number of the northern Black ministers became influential in politics and in protest.[5]

Ghettoization had produced an urban Black population with in-creasing frustration and anger over being crowded into substan-dard housing and being trapped in the cycle of poor schooling, underemployment and poverty. From the next phase in the north-ern stream would emerge a philosophy focusing this anger and causing a sweeping cultural change—a change which would fan the flames of this smoldering population into an urban eruption.

Meanwhile, in the South, cultural forces were already converg-ing to usher in the next *southern* phase. Chapter seven will focus attention on this strategic phase and its heroic spokesman.

Chapter 7

"De Lawd"

BUILT ON THE RUINS of the Neo-Colored phase and based in the Black church, another southern strategy emerged. In its early days the Neo-Negro strategy was an attempt to bring to the South the same level of freedom which Blacks in the North seemed to enjoy. Desegregation was the goal. This phase came to the fore shortly after the Supreme Court in 1954 ruled that segregation was unconstitutional. It quickly became obvious, however, that desegregation was not going to come about through the goodness of people's hearts. We had learned through the Neo-Colored and the Negro phases that, as far as we were concerned, White humanism was on its deathbed. The only way for us to enter the American mainstream was through *law*.

The Spirit of the Time

We had no idea how to mobilize the kind of cultural power needed to overcome hard-core Jim-Crowism and legally break the patterns of segregation. The Neo-Negro consensus expressed a belief that once we achieved desegregation, racial tension would subside. Ignorance on which racial prejudice was based would be wiped out through understanding. "Men often hate each other because they fear each other; they fear each other because they do not know each other; they do not know each other because they cannot communicate; they cannot communicate because they are separated."[1] The stage was set for a new movement to meet the challenge. It was the right time.

> On December 1, 1955, an attractive Negro seamstress, Mrs. Rosa Parks, boarded the Cleveland Avenue bus in downtown Montgomery [Alabama]. She was returning home after her regular day's work in a leading department store. Tired from long hours on her feet, Mrs. Parks sat down in the first seat behind the section reserved for whites. Not long after she took her seat, the bus operator ordered her, along with three other Negro passengers, to move back in order to accommodate boarding white passengers. By this time every seat in the bus was taken. This meant that if Mrs. Parks followed the driver's command she would have to stand while a white male passenger, who had just boarded the bus, would sit. The other three Negro passengers immediately complied with the driver's request. But Mrs. Parks quietly refused. The result was her arrest. . . .
>
> She was anchored to that seat by the accumulated indignities of days gone by and the boundless aspirations of generations yet unborn. She was a victim of both the forces of history and the forces of destiny. She had been tracked down by the *Zeitgeist*— the spirit of the time.[2]

This was the first of a sequence of events which would consolidate and bring to national attention the Neo-Negro phase of Black history. The arrest of Mrs. Parks sent waves of outrage throughout the Black community of Montgomery. For the first time in anybody's memory, the Black community was of one mind as to what to do about the situation. This oneness was recognized at the meeting of Montgomery's Black ministers: " . . . something unusual was about to happen."[3]

Though the meeting lacked coherence, no one present questioned the validity of the proposed response: a bus boycott. Almost all the influential Black ministers were present at that meeting, and they agreed to speak to their congregations on Sunday morning about the proposed boycott. A citywide meeting was planned for Monday night, December 5, to determine how long they would refuse to ride the buses.

The first day of the boycott was a total success. As one eyewitness described it,

> All day long it continued. . . . During the rush hours the sidewalks were crowded with laborers and domestic workers, many of them well past middle age, trudging patiently to their jobs and home again, sometimes as much as twelve miles. They knew why they walked, and the knowledge was evident in the way they carried themselves. And as I watched them I knew that there is nothing more majestic than the determined courage of individuals willing to suffer and sacrifice for their freedom and dignity.[4]

The Right Man   Present at the ministers' meeting that night of Mrs. Parks's arrest was a young preacher who had just finished his Ph.D. thesis. He had devoted a great deal of time to its writing and was looking forward to giving more attention to his church work. Because of this, he turned down an opportunity to run for president of the local chapter of the National Association for the Advancement of Colored People (NAACP). But now he was caught by the current of history: leadership for the protest had to be chosen.

> As soon as [Roy] Bennett had opened the nominations for president, Rufus Lewis spoke from the far corner of the room: "Mr. Chairman, I would like to nominate Reverend M. L. King for president." The motion was seconded and carried, and in a matter of minutes I was unanimously elected.

The action had caught me unawares. It had happened so quickly that I did not even have time to think it through. It is probable that if I had, I would have declined the nomination.[5] Events had moved too fast. It was unanimously agreed that the protest should continue until certain demands were met. These demands were drawn up in the form of a resolution to be presented at the December 5 meeting for approval. Dr. King was to make the main address.

"I was now almost overcome, obsessed by a feeling of inadequacy," confessed Dr. King. He had nowhere to turn but to God, "whose matchless strength stands over against the frailties and inadequacies of human nature."[6] He prayed for guidance.

I faced a new and sobering dilemma: How could I make a speech that would be militant enough to keep my people aroused to positive action and yet moderate enough to keep this fervor within controllable and Christian bounds? . . . Could the militant and the moderate be combined in a single speech?

I decided that I had to face the challenge head on, and attempt to combine two apparent irreconcilables. I would seek to arouse the group to action by insisting that their self-respect was at stake and that if they accepted such injustices without protesting, they would betray their own sense of dignity and the eternal edicts of God Himself. But I would balance this with a strong affirmation of the Christian doctrine of love.[7]

In accepting the responsibility of spokesman, Dr. King found his mind being "driven back to the Sermon on the Mount and the Gandhian method of nonviolent resistance. This principle became the guiding light of our movement. Christ furnished the spirit and motivation and [Mahatma] Gandhi furnished the method."[8]

When Monday night came, the cars and people were lined up as far as the eye could see. They were all headed to the meeting. With TV cameras running, Dr. Martin Luther King, Jr., began to deliver a speech that would change the course of history. Without referring to notes, he told the story of what happened to Mrs. Parks. Then he reviewed the long history of abuses that Black citizens had experienced on the city buses. He continued:

But there comes a time that people get tired. We are here this
evening to say to those who have mistreated us so long that we
are tired—tired of being segregated and humiliated; tired of being
kicked about by the brutal feet of oppression. We had no alternative but to protest. For many years, we have shown amazing
patience. We have sometimes given our white brothers the feeling that we liked the way we were being treated. But we come
here tonight to be saved from that patience that makes us patient
with anything less than freedom and justice. . . .

Our method will be that of persuasion, not coercion. . . . Our
actions must be guided by the deepest principles of our Christian
faith. Love must be our regulating ideal. Once again we must
hear the words of Jesus echoing across the centuries: "Love your
enemies, bless them that curse you, and pray for them that de-
spitefully use you." If we fail to do this our protest will end up as
a meaningless drama on the stage of history, and its memory will
be shrouded with the ugly garments of shame. In spite of the mistreatment that we have confronted we must not become bitter
and end up by hating our white brothers. As Booker T. Washington said, "Let no man pull you so low as to make you hate him."

If you will protest courageously, and yet with dignity and
Christian love, when the history books are written in future
generations, the historians will have to pause and say, "There
lived a great people—a black people—who injected new meaning and dignity in the veins of civilization." This is our challenge and our overwhelming responsibility.[9]

As King sat listening to the long applause, he realized that his
speech had evoked more response than any speech or sermon he
had ever delivered, and yet it was virtually unprepared. He came to
realize for the first time what the older preachers meant when they
said, "Open your mouth and God will speak for you."[10]

To parallel Mordecai's statement to Queen Esther (Esther 4:14):
If Martin had kept quiet at that time, help would have come from
another quarter. But King was ready at the right time, and he gave

the people a message they could act upon.

The Right Message Nonviolent protest was the tool King introduced in Montgomery. Through the years he became more and more convinced of the power of nonviolence to bring about justice.

Montgomery became a testing ground, a crucible. Truth force and love force consolidated in Black culture as "soul force." In Montgomery were thousands of Black folks whose "feets was tired" but whose "souls was at rest"—and empty buses. White folks frequently harassed them, while the KKK stirred up violence. The result after 384 days was the birth of a powerful movement which overflowed from the Montgomery crucible throughout Alabama, the South, the United States and, ultimately, to the ends of the earth.

What was it that gave the civil-rights movement and its main prophet the uncanny power to transform a downtrodden people into a mighty army, to bring the most powerful government on earth to its knees in repentance?

To many Whites in the South who thought that their "Coloreds" were happy with the status quo and well cared for, the civil-rights movement was incomprehensible. It caught them completely off-guard. Many Whites expressed complete bewilderment at the transformation of Black folks as they became caught up with the new southern winds which were beginning to blow down the mighty citadels of segregation. "I dawn't unda-stay'en what's goin' awn. T's like some'mm dun jumped int-a awva nigras ova' night."

Many have tried to explain the civil-rights movement merely as a people movement, but it doesn't work. As Brother Martin himself explained, this movement, which suddenly catapulted him into worldwide recognition, cannot be explained without God. In 1958 he wrote:

> ... every rational explanation breaks down at some point. There is something about the protest that is suprarational; it cannot be explained without a divine dimension.... God still works through history His wonders to perform. It seems as though God had decided to use Montgomery as the proving ground for the

struggle and triumph of freedom and justice in America. And what better place for it than the leading symbol of the Old South? It is one of the splendid ironies of our day that Montgomery, the Cradle of the Confederacy, is being transformed into Montgomery, the cradle of freedom and justice.

... in the first days of the protest none of these expressions was mentioned; the phrase most often heard was "Christian love." It was the Sermon on the Mount, rather than a doctrine of passive resistance, that initially inspired the Negroes of Montgomery to dignified social action. It was Jesus of Nazareth that stirred the Negroes to protest with the creative weapon of love.[11]

A Tale of One City

As early as the post-World War 2 years several Black leaders had begun to contemplate the significance of 1963, the one-hundred-year anniversary of the Emancipation Proclamation. It was painfully obvious to them that after all these years of legal freedom, we were still under the yoke of racism. Many leaders began to call for the full implementation of the Fourteenth and Fifteenth Amendments. Montgomery had awakened the nation, and now "Free by 63" became the rally cry, echoing through the Black nation during the 1950s and into the early 1960s. Thus our focus was on 1963. King wrote,

Yet not all of these forces conjoined could have brought about the massive and largely bloodless Revolution of 1963 if there had not been at hand a philosophy and a method worthy of its goals. Nonviolent direct action did not originate in America, but it found its natural home in this land, where refusal to cooperate with injustice was an ancient and honorable tradition and where Christian forgiveness was written into the minds and hearts of good men. Tested in Montgomery during the winter of 1955-56, and toughened throughout the South in the eight ensuing years, nonviolent resistance had become, by 1963, the logical force in the greatest mass-action crusade for freedom that has ever occurred in American history.[12]

Nowhere was this crusade for freedom in 1963 seen more clearly than in Birmingham, Alabama. Birmingham's brutal system of segregation was well known throughout the South. It had thoroughly intimidated all who lived under its yoke. Nowhere but in the Birmingham of Eugene "Bull" Connor, the public safety commissioner, was the power of soul force so visibly demonstrated.

In Connor's Birmingham, the silent password was fear. It was a fear not only on the part of the black oppressed, but also in the hearts of the white oppressors. Guilt was a part of their fear. There was also the dread of change, that all too prevalent fear which hounds those whose attitudes have been hardened by the long winter of reaction. Many were apprehensive of social ostracism. Certainly Birmingham had its white moderates who disapproved of Bull Connor's tactics. Certainly Birmingham had its decent white citizens who privately deplored the maltreatment of Negroes. But they remained publicly silent. It was a silence born of fear—fear of social, political and economic reprisals. The ultimate tragedy of Birmingham was not the brutality of bad people, but the silence of the good people.[13]

Lessons from Birmingham   The movement in Birmingham can teach us a number of things. It teaches us about ethics. King, along with hundreds of others, had been arrested for demonstrating against segregation. In his "Letter from Birmingham Jail," King not only answered his critics, but he provided a definitive ethical basis for the whole civil-rights movement, an apologetic we will discuss later.[14] Birmingham demonstrated that to go to jail in the cause of freedom was both an honor and a spiritual experience. Behind the Birmingham bars, the older participants led Bible studies which spoke to the events transpiring about them. They led the demonstrators in prayer and thanksgiving, for they could see the hand of God at work in their midst. Thus the theological dynamic of the Black church was part of the very fabric of the Birmingham event.

An important part of the mass meetings was the freedom songs. In a sense the freedom songs are the soul of the movement. They are more than just incantations of clever phrases designed to invigorate a campaign; they are as old as the history of the Negro in America. They are adaptations of the songs the slaves sang— the sorrow songs, the shouts for joy, the battle hymns and the anthems of our movement. I have heard people talk of their beat and rhythm, but we in the movement are as inspired by their words. "Woke Up This Morning with My Mind Stayed on Freedom" is a sentence that needs no music to make its point. We sing the freedom songs today for the same reason the slaves sang them, because we too are in bondage and the songs add hope to our determination that "We shall overcome, Black and white together, We shall overcome someday."

I have stood in a meeting with hundreds of youngsters and joined in while they sang "Ain't Gonna Let Nobody Turn Me 'Round." It is not a song; it is a resolve. A few minutes later, I have seen those same youngsters refuse to turn around from the onrush of a police dog, refuse to turn around before a pugnacious Bull Connor in command of men armed with power hoses. These songs bind us together, give us courage together, help us to march together.[15]

The Red Sea   The drama reached a powerful climax when those under the direct authority of Bull Connor were moved by the Spirit to obey God rather than man. Connor became so frustrated that he was driven to the point of frenzy as the whole world looked on.

It was a Sunday afternoon, when several hundred Birmingham Negroes had determined to hold a prayer meeting near the city jail. They gathered at the New Pilgrim Baptist Church and began an orderly march. Bull Connor ordered out the police dogs and fire hoses. When the marchers approached the border between the white and Negro areas, Connor ordered them to turn back. The Reverend Charles Billups, who was leading the march, politely refused.

We asked everybody to get down on their knees. And they got down on their knees in their Easter Sunday go to meet'n [clothes]. Somebody just started praying in these old traditional chants of the black community [the theological dynamic]. Peo-

ple were moaning, crying and praying.... Bull Connor was
totally difficult and said he was going to throw us all in jail.

All of a sudden some old lady got up and said "God is with
this movement, we goin' on to the jail." She got up and everybody started [getting up].

Enraged, Bull Connor whirled on his men and shouted:
"Dammit. Turn on the hoses."

What happened in the next thirty seconds was one of the most
fantastic events of the Birmingham story. Bull Connor's men,
their deadly hoses poised for action, stood facing the marchers.

If they had turned [the hoses] on, the pressure from that close
distance would have broken people's ribs. Bull Connor was
[yelling], "Stop 'em, Stop 'em!!!"

The marchers, many of them [still] on their knees, stared
back, unafraid and unmoving. Slowly the Negroes stood up and
began to advance.

These firemen... who really didn't know any better, had
been so moved by this experience, that... they never turned
the hoses on.

Connor's men, as though hypnotized, fell back, their hoses
sagging uselessly in their hands while several hundred Negroes
marched past them.

The dogs that had been straining at the leash, jumping at us,
all of a sudden just stopped, and we walked right on through.
And somebody hollered out, "Great God Almighty done parted
the Red Sea one more time!!"[16]

That broke the back of segregation in Birmingham. It brought the
White leaders to the conference table and, in the end, even the
opposition could not withstand the power of soul force.

Birmingham taught us not only about ethics and the dynamic of
the situation, but about people. The movement had a profound
effect on Blacks who had previously been intimidated. There was
a new spirit in the air. King wrote of the oppressed at this time:

When, for decades, you have been able to make a man com-
promise his manhood by threatening him with a cruel and un-

just punishment, and when suddenly he turns upon you and says: "Punish me. I do not deserve it. But because I do not deserve it, I will accept it so that the world will know that I am right and you are wrong," you hardly know what to do. You feel defeated and secretly ashamed. You know that this man is as good a man as you are; that from some mysterious source he has found the courage and the conviction to meet physical force with soul force.[17]

Of the effect on the oppressor King wrote:

Nonviolent resistance paralyzed and confused the power structures against which it was directed. The brutality with which officials would have quelled the black individual became impotent when it could not be pursued with stealth and remain unobserved. It was caught—as a fugitive from a penitentiary is often caught—in gigantic circling spotlights. It was imprisoned in a luminous glare revealing the naked truth to the whole world.[18]

What happened in Birmingham was a classical confrontation between actions derived from righteousness and those derived from oppression. It was an ethical debate carried out in the streets. "Discernment can come about in unexpected ways. It may, of course, come about in expected ways: perhaps a verse of Scripture coming to mind, perhaps a fact of experience not noticed before.... But, since one may know all the verses, and all the facts, without knowing the *patterns,* often the insight will come in odd ways."[19]

The nonviolent demonstrations dramatized the teachings of Jesus. Those who participated in the drama were walking in the shoes of Jesus and proclaiming his Word through their actions. Those who opposed the demonstrations found themselves trying to hold back the same Word of God which brought forth the universe and upholds it.

Ethical discourse is never merely a matter of setting forth facts and verses. In an ethical debate, one or both parties may be very knowledgeable about Scripture and experience, but unable to make the connections because of immaturity.

Thus, it is useful, not only to reason, but also to tell stories, to pray, to sing, to share analogies, to do odd things for "shock value" (Ezekiel), to teach by example.[20]

Teaching by example was the essence of the Birmingham experience for the demonstrators. Shock value came when the opposition saw their own bigotry and violence exposed in plain sight to the world.

White America was forced to face the ugly facts of life as the Negro thrust himself into the consciousness of the country, and dramatized his grievances on a thousand brightly lighted stages. No period in American history, save the Civil War and the Reconstruction, records such breadth and depth to the Negro's drive to alter his life. No period records so many thaws in the frozen patterns of segregation.[21]

King had become the leader, motivator, spokesman and focus of this dramatic movement. Who was this voice from the South?

"We Didn't Know Who You Was"

Martin Luther King, Jr., was ideal for the role assigned to him by the Lord of history. His character was impeccable, his dedication and brilliance deep-rooted. These traits made him highly respected in the Black community.

Mayor Andrew Young, former U. N. Ambassador, recalls, "I think he made no distinctions between people. He was not interested in their education. He saw straight through to the heart of a human being, and that was where he tried to relate to people. . . . He was so basically humble and unassuming and yet he was so obviously talented. The man would become transformed once he got behind a pulpit and [people] could see the brilliance of his leadership."[22] This is why those close to King affectionately called him "De Lawd."

A Time of Training   King did not go to an evangelical seminary. Had he applied to one, he quite possibly would have been rejected on racial grounds. But since our Lord is sovereign over history, King received the preparation needed to become the leader, theo-

74 Beyond Liberation

logian and prophet of the civil-rights movement.

Having been raised in a strict fundamentalist tradition, in his senior year at Crozer Seminary (where he earned an M.Div.) King began to journey through new doctrinal lands. But the theological dynamic was alive in this third-generation preacher, providing "theological antibodies" against the infections of all that he would study—liberalism, neo-orthodoxy and, later, existentialism. His Black church background had equipped him to "eat the fish and spit out the bones."

Although King did not accept everything liberalism encompassed, he was impressed with its intellectual vigor, something he had never found in fundamentalism. But he questioned the liberal doctrine that humanity is basically good. The more he "observed the tragedies of history and man's shameful inclination to take the low road," the more he came to see the depths of sin. Liberalism for Dr. King was "all too sentimental concerning human nature and it leaned toward false idealism." Liberalism had optimistically overlooked "the glaring reality of collective evil" and "the fact that reason was darkened by sin."

King found neo-orthodoxy to be "a helpful corrective for a sentimental liberalism," but "it did not provide an answer to basic questions." Where liberalism "was too optimistic concerning human nature, neo-orthodoxy was too pessimistic." For him, neo-orthodoxy went too far in "stressing a God who was hidden, unknown, and 'wholly other.' " Existentialism was the next step in his intellectual journey, but King acknowledged that "the ultimate Christian answer could not be found in existential assertions."

Social ethics increasingly commanded his interest. In his early teens King had been very concerned about the problem of racial injustice. During his doctoral studies at Boston University Divinity School, the "social gospel" expressed by Walter Rauschenbusch left an indelible imprint on King's thinking. Brother Martin never, however, bought Rauschenbusch's "unwarranted optimism concerning human nature." Rauschenbusch also came "perilously close to identifying the Kingdom of God with a particular social and economic system." This King vigorously opposed. He believed that "the gospel at its best deals with the whole man, not only his soul but also his body, not only his spiritual well-being but also his material well-being." In other words, "a religion that professes a concern for the souls of men and is not equally concerned about the slums that damn them, the economic conditions that strangle them, and the social conditions that cripple them, is a spiritually moribund religion."

After studying several social and ethical theories, Brother Martin almost despaired of the power of love to solve social problems. "The turn-the-other-cheek and the love-your-enemies philosophies are valid," he felt, "only when individuals are in conflict with other individuals; when racial groups and nations are in conflict, a more realistic approach is necessary."[23]

It all came together for him in the next stage of his journey. He explains:

> I was introduced to the life and teachings of Mahatma Gandhi. As I read his works I became deeply fascinated by his campaigns of nonviolent resistance. The whole Gandhian concept of *satyagraha* (*satya* is truth which equals love and *graha* is force; *satyagraha* thus means truth-force or love-force) was profoundly significant to me. As I delved deeper into the philosophy of Gandhi, my skepticism concerning the power of love gradually diminished, and I came to see for the first time that the Christian doctrine of love, operating through the Gandhian method of nonviolence, is one of the most potent weapons available to an oppressed people in their struggle for freedom.[24]

A Blinded Church King was misunderstood by many in both the Black community and the White. Most acute and embarrassing of these misunderstandings, however, were those of the so-called Bible-believing community. King's theological dynamic gave him a biblical message and method which neither conformed to the White conservative agenda nor to the White liberal agenda.

Sadly, many White evangelical, fundamentalist and Reformed churches were caught sleeping with no oil in their lamps at the outbreak of this move of God in the land. They had evidently been lulled to sleep by a defective view of theology and culture. They failed to distinguish between White standards and scriptural standards. Their theology had led them to a preoccupation with private salvation.

The importance of personal salvation should never be diminished. But the whole council of God revealed in the Scriptures goes far beyond the scope of the private realm. According to God's Word, even salvation itself finds its significance in terms of a much larger picture—namely, the praise of God's glory (Eph 1—2). But many leading evangelicals never came to grips with the big picture of God's purposes. They never saw the broad cultural implications of the Great Commission. This is why their Christianity never had application beyond the private aspects of life. Many believed that America's racial injustices would fade away merely through individuals' having conversion experiences. This naive view completely ignored the patterns of racism that had been woven into the American system.

The fundamentalist reaction was much harsher. Fundamentalists and right-wing politicians branded this movement and King as "communistic." Though there was no evidence for such allegations, the label effectively scared off some potential supporters. The civil-rights movement and the words of King were beginning to strike at the very root of the White Christianity-ism which supported the political, economic and social system in which they had a vested interest.

Many fundamentalists and evangelicals saw the message of Brother Martin as an experience in futility in light of the total dichotomy between the sweet by-and-by and the nasty "now-and-now."[25] They saw Dr. King as absurdly "bothering to polish the brass and rearrange the furniture on the Titanic." According to them, "he should have been getting people 'saved' in these 'last days' and not been concerned with eating at lunch counters."

On the other hand, those in the Reformed church community, who pride themselves on having a wholistic theology, were better equipped to understand the phenomena of Brother Martin. King was trying to bring the reality of the biblical world and life view to bear on the real problems in society, such as racism and segregation. He firmly believed that history was neither autonomous nor a chance occurrence of events, but that God was sovereign over all things. He believed in the power of the Spirit of God to quicken people to respond positively to the Word. King was firmly rooted in the life of the church and saw the kingdom of God as having a broad sphere of influence in its theology and ethics. Yet the Reformed Christians who shared his outlook did not recognize him. They were caught in the "paralysis of analysis."[26]

When King listed the churches which endorsed the civil-rights movement, the so-called Bible-believing churches were conspicuously absent.[27] Was it too much to expect them to recognize the ethical and theological nature of the movement when it was at its peak?

Without input from the Black community the White church was unable to see the structural sin in the American system. Reformed thinkers like J. Marcellus Kik who expressed themselves on the subject of the ethical application of theology to social problems tended to be negative.[28] Other thinkers said things like "Immediate integration would be destructive to Blacks and Whites alike," or "The problems of racism will eventually disappear under the present system of preaching the Word." The same arguments are offered today by portions of the Dutch Reformed Church in South Africa.

Thus the mainline, Bible-believing community generally misunderstood the significance of King—the fundamentalists and evangelicals primarily because of their defective theological position and the Reformed Christians primarily because of their defective cultural position.

This blindness in the conservative churches was due in part to the nature of Western theology itself. It had developed under the challenge of unbelieving philosophy and science, and thus it was much more concerned with *epistemological* issues (what we

should know about God) than with ethical ones (how we should
obey God). The White church had generally been absent from the
Black community for almost a hundred years, and Brother Martin
was the product of the Black church—a church with a distinctly
different growth and flavor. Hence, just as the kingdom of God
had caught the scribes and Pharisees unawares, so the civil-rights
movement caught the predominantly White, Bible-believing communities unawares. Ironically, the liberals, who had apparently
departed from God's written Word, were able to recognize this
move of God better than those who were supposed to be committed
to God's Word.

Brother Martin had been tracked down by the spirit of the time.
He had been tracked down by the Spirit of God operating in our
lives and times by the grace of God—a grace rooted in Jesus Christ
(Jn 1:16). It is that same Spirit which has been at work throughout
history in general, and in Black history in particular. It is that same
Spirit of grace which brought us through Montgomery in 1955-56
and to the pinnacle of the civil-rights movement in the triumph in
Birmingham and in the March on Washington in the summer of
1963.

"It is an axiom of social change that no revolution can take place
without a methodology suited to the circumstances of the period."[29] Nonviolence was the ideal methodology for the southern,
Neo-Negro strategy given the overwhelming power of the forces
arrayed against our people. Many had offered violent strategies,
but the power of the Word of God dramatized in the streets of the
South proved far more powerful than all the forces of segregation
put together.

The Word Applied
We cannot discuss the civil-rights movement without discussing
theology. But what is theology and why were so many theologians
caught napping by this movement?

Theology itself has been traditionally defined as "the study of
God." Since the study of God would be impossible without his

Word, we can define theology as "the application of God's Word to all areas of life,"[30] including the study of God.

Another theological area of concern has been the defense of the faith, historically called apologetics. In line with our broader perspective on theology, apologetics would be best defined as "the application of God's Word to controversy."[31] We have already noted that historic Black theology has been more ethical than epistemological. "Ethics is not a branch of theology but *equivalent to theology* because all theology answers ethical questions."[32] The civil-rights movement applied the theological dynamic to the controversy of southern injustice. Thus, what we had in King's message was the best example to date of an *ethics apologetic.* It had individual, collective and social implications.

Pointing to Jesus The center of this ethics apologetic was the Sermon on the Mount. Sadly, the Sermon on the Mount had been relegated to a bygone age by some Bible-believing Christians, while others simply never got around to its social implications. But King did. King was an ethics apologist after the order of an Old Testament prophet. He called the United States to repentance and obedience to God.

Brother Martin's message separated the wheat from the tares. He gave us a vehicle for rediscovering the ethical dimensions of "kingdom life" (for example, Is 58; Mt 7:21-27; 25:34-46). He reminded us that the judgment of God had ethical aspects (Lk 6:20-31) which were to be worked out in society (Is 2:1-5; Lk 4:18-19).

King looked for God's answer to racial injustice. Fundamentalism did not have it; and though he learned some valuable things from fundamentalism, he did not remain a fundamentalist. Liberalism did not have it; and though he learned some valuable things from liberalism, he did not become a liberal. Neo-orthodoxy did not have it; and though he learned some valuable things from neo-orthodoxy, he did not become neo-orthodox. Evangelicalism did not have it; and because evangelicalism stayed within its comfortable non-Black cultural niche, he did not become an evangelical. Reformed theology could have had it, but its theologians stayed within the parameters of their traditional confessions. Gandhi had discovered some of the answers and offered them to Brother Martin.

Though Mahatma Gandhi, a Hindu, equipped King with a method, King never bought into the religion of Hinduism. Brother Martin was too thoroughly saturated with the Black theological dynamic, the integration point for all he learned.

We must remember that the primary test of orthodoxy in the historic Black church is different from what it is in predominantly White, conservative church circles. In White culture the test tends to be *conceptual*, that is, how one articulates his theology in confessions, creeds or statements of faith. In the Black church this test tends to be *existential*, that is, how well one personally knows God or uses the theological dynamic. According to Scripture there is a third test which is *situational*, that is, how sensitive and committed one is to actualizing the truth of God's Word, or how obedient he is to the ethical implications of Christ's teachings.

We must also remember that in Scripture orthodoxy is most often measured on ethical grounds. While most in the Bible-believing community are more consistent to Scripture conceptually than ethically, Dr. King was perhaps more consistent to Scripture ethically than conceptually. From a conceptual perspective Brother Martin appeared to be less than orthodox; from an ethical perspective, however, many Bible-believing Christians appear less than orthodox. The ideal for all of us should be total scriptural consistency in all aspects of faith.

King was often criticized for trying to get Black non-Christians to be nonviolent and White non-Christians to obey Jesus' words by implementing the golden rule. However, this criticism is based on a faulty view of the Christian's duty in this fallen world. As Cornelius VanTil says, we are called both to restrain sin and to destroy its consequences in this world as much as may be possible.

It is our duty not only to seek to destroy evil in ourselves and in our fellow Christians, but it is our further duty to seek to destroy evil in all our fellow men. It may be, humanly speaking, hopeless in some instances that we should succeed in bringing them to Christ. This does not absolve us, however, from seeking to restrain their sins to some extent for this life. We must be active first of all in the field of special grace, but we also have a task to perform with respect to the destruction of evil in the field of common grace.

Still further we must note that our task with respect to the destruction of evil is not done if we have sought to fight sin itself everywhere we see it. We have the further obligation to destroy the consequences of sin in this world as far as we can. We must do good to all men, especially to those of the household of faith. To help relieve something of the sufferings of the creatures of God is our privilege and our task.[33]

Dr. King was also criticized for not preaching the full gospel and not getting people saved. But we can't always preach the gospel at fifty-five miles an hour. When road and weather conditions are bad, we have to slow down to a safe or understandable speed. In the case of the civil-rights movement, the goal was to eliminate segregation (to apply the gospel at five miles per hour). How did the civil-rights movement relate to the gospel? Segregation points to racism; racism points to human depravity; depravity points to human rebellion against God; rebellion brings God's judgment and wrath; judgment points to our need for salvation, and our need for salvation points to Jesus Christ, our only hope for it. Martin Luther King, Jr., applied the Word of God to the evils manifested in society without letting us forget that Jesus was the ultimate fulfillment of the civil-rights movement.

Agenda for Justice
The only real problem with the theological dynamic had been its limited application to the social problems faced by Black America. Until the time of Dr. King, its only social application was a *passive* one—survival and accommodation to the atrocities of racism. King gave us a fresh and aggressive application of the dynamic to the southern cause of justice. No one could remain neutral to its ethical and social implications. Our people had the will to resist oppres-

sion but they had not had the method. God raised up Brother Martin to give us that method, renewing our will to resist. God's grace pervaded this important phase of our quest. If the meaning of the Black nation's history is rooted in searching for God (Acts 17:26-28), then Dr. Martin Luther King's ethics apologetic was a great stride in that direction.

Once the back of legal segregation was broken, there was truly cause for celebration. The federal government responded to the call to repentance with the passage of the civil-rights and voting-rights bills, along with the establishment of the Commission on Civil Rights to ensure the implementation of these laws. Black people were now more able to pursue freedom and dignity. We could now broaden our quest for true personhood—a status we had hoped to find in the melting pot.

For the first time a few "visible" Black people actually entered the melting pot and began to report back what life was like inside. And the story was not very promising. It was not the freedom and dignity we were looking for; it was a rat race. In mainstream life, Black culture was still unacceptable, so many who "integrated" found that they could not enter authentically. Integration for them meant that they had to "give up their identity and deny their heritage."[34] What we thought of as the promised land was in sight— but it was a desert.

For the ghettoized masses who were alienated from the institutions of America, mere access to the melting pot made little difference. Louis E. Lomax explained what had happened:

By marching, singing, praying and suffering, Martin Luther King let America out of the prison of legal segregation. Only after the prison walls fell was it fully laid bare that the inmates of segregation had been maimed for life. Their tortured souls could be heard groaning in agony and despair from Mississippi to Cleveland's Hough, from Georgia to Watts, from Alabama to Harlem. King . . . had opened the door but the newly freed men were too crippled by experience to walk in.[35]

Though freedom and dignity were not to be found in the melting pot, we learned several things from the Neo-Negro phase. First, we discovered how essential the soul dynamic was for our cause, as evidenced by its profound effect not only on Black folks but on America at large. Second, we learned that segregation, though a form of oppression, was not the total picture of oppression, and that desegregation, though a fruit of liberation, was not the total picture of liberation; for racism in the hearts of people is not negated by laws. Third, the cultural price of entering the melting pot was too high; and, in fact, the melting pot system could never produce freedom and dignity for our people.

Most of us felt a gnawing within our guts as we came to realize the truth which a fiery young man superbly articulated:

It's impossible for a chicken to produce a duck egg—even though they both belong to the same family of fowl. A chicken just doesn't have it within its system to produce a duck egg. It can't do it. It can only produce according to what that particular system was constructed to produce. The system in this country cannot produce freedom for an Afro-American. It is impossible for this system, this economic system, this political system, this social system, this system, period. It's impossible for this system, as it stands, to produce freedom right now for the black man in this country.

And if ever a chicken did produce a duck egg, I'm quite sure you would say it was certainly a revolutionary chicken![36]

Post-Martin Crisis Those who followed Brother Martin have tried to continue his work in two ways. Some looked to the institutions that had originally responded to the civil-rights movement as vehicles to advance our people. Among these groups were the Southern Christian Leadership Conference (SCLC), which was founded by King himself; Operation Breadbasket, a branch of SCLC; Operation PUSH (People United to Save Humanity); the Urban League and the NAACP. A second group looked to the nonviolent strategy and the memory of Brother Martin as the keys to continuing progress. The Martin Luther King, Jr., Center for Social Change, headed by Mrs. Coretta Scott King, represents this perspective.

All these groups have contributed to our people since the assassination of Brother Martin in 1968, but they lack the prophetic power possessed by King. Some lack his power because they have tied in too closely with the federal government. We can be thankful for the response of the federal government, but we should not have declared a total victory. Other American institutions also have racist structures that need to be reformed: schools, clubs, churches and labor unions, to name a few. And other levels of government still need to be tackled by the civil-rights movement. State and local governments have proven themselves incapable of guarding the rights of Black people. While politically liberal politicians have worked to make the federal government a watchdog over the racial practices of lower levels of government, conservatives have been fighting to take such watchdog power away from Washington. Events since 1980 have borne out our need to be guaranteed freedom through state and local structures also, and not to depend on the federal government.

While King looked to nonviolence as a means of unleashing the power of God, his followers looked to the strategy of nonviolence itself as the answer. Hence they lack King's prophetic power. We can be thankful for the method of nonviolence, but nonviolence was not the force. Nonviolence did not have the power to change structures because it was nonviolent; its strength was derived from God. American culture, like all cultures, has a way of accommodating itself to new expressions of truth the way the human body accommodates itself to dope. With the first injection comes an initial, blissful "rush"; but with succeeding injections and addiction an increasing numbness sets in, and the body no longer responds. This was the case with nonviolence. Initially it was a powerful means of cultural discipleship, but as time passed and the American culture became acclimated to it, numbness crept in. The shock value was lost. We needed new methods of applying God's Word and power.

King was concerned about God's righteousness and justice wherever they were needed. He showed us that God's Word could be applied to other social issues, like the Vietnam War and hunger. He saw that biblical ethics must be applied to every area of life. When King took aim at the war, many thought he had abandoned the cause of Black people. When he planned the Poor People's March on Washington, many did not understand why the issue was poverty, not just racism. Time has vindicated him. Ultimately it is not Black versus White, it is justice versus injustice, Haves versus Have-nots. Today even those in the middle class are beginning to feel themselves sliding toward being Have-nots. As long as King only talked about Blacks, he was relatively safe, but when he began to pull poor Whites and poor Blacks together he became a threat to the power and wealth elite. If he had been allowed to live, he might have even been able to articulate the frustrations of today's shrinking middle class. Thus Brother Martin could have been a prophet of a sizable slice of America. This would have been a formidable challenge but it was never allowed to materialize.

We can thank God for Martin Luther King, Jr., and for his ethics apologetic, which gave God's worldwide church a valuable tool for making disciples of all nations. Yes, we can be thankful for this prophet who had a love ethic like Jesus', a cultural brilliance like Paul's, a poetic speech like Jeremiah's, an agenda for justice like Amos's, a direct-action drama like Ezekiel's and a mode of leadership like Moses'. God had spoken to Brother Martin:

God has spoken to me, and I'm not going to run from the responsibility!

May mean going through the floods and through the waters, but I'm going if it means that!

May mean going through the storms and the winds, but I'm going, if it means that!

May mean going to jail, but I'm going if it means that!

It may even mean physical death, but if it means that I will die standing up for the freedom of my people!

God has spoken to me![37]

Chapter 8

"A Shining Prince"

O NCE WE HAD UNCOVERED the well-kept secret that freedom and dignity were not to be found in the melting pot, many began to rethink the whole direction of the quest. Rumblings of discontent increased among the more militant northern thinkers during the later stages of the civil-rights movement. They were among the first to become disenchanted with nonviolence; for example, they condemned King's action during the "Battle of Selma" (1964). Eldridge Cleaver considered this incident the beginning of the end of the civil-rights movement:

[Dr. King] denied history a great moment, never to be recaptured, when he turned tail on the Edmund Pettus Bridge and refused to all those whites behind him what they had traveled thousands of miles to receive. If the police had turned them back by force, all those nuns, priests, rabbis, preachers, and distinguished ladies and gentlemen old and young—as they had done the Negroes a week earlier—the violence and brutality of the system would have been ruthlessly exposed. Or if, seeing King determined to lead them on to Montgomery, the troopers had stepped aside to avoid precisely the confrontation that Washington would not have tolerated, it would have signaled the capitulation of the militant white South. As it turned out, the March on Montgomery was a show of somewhat dim luster, stage-managed by the Establishment.[1]

Shock Waves

From that time on some of the more militant marchers began to chant "Black Power, Black Power!" During the Memphis-to-Jackson march Stokely Carmichael, the new leader of the Student Nonviolent Coordinating Committee (SNCC), openly challenged Dr. King to take a stand for Black Power.[2]

Shock waves spread across America. A consciousness change was taking place among the new Black leaders, signaling the beginning of the Black phase. With it White humanism was dead and buried, and Black humanism was born. Just as the death of Reconstruction in 1877 marked the beginning of the melting pot era, so the Black phase marked its end. For the first time White society began to deal with us on our terms or mutually acceptable terms.

During this transitional stage of our history, all color gradation in our thinking melted. We were all "Black." We began to discover the richness of our heritage, and the new discoveries made us acutely aware that the American system had "run a number on us." As the authors of *What Color Is Your God?* say, this new consciousness was

> the bold assertion of the fact that the humanity of Blacks is a non-negotiable, indisputable reality. The humanity of Black people *is!*

[It was] *initially* the psychological realization that White op-
pressive, dehumanizing institutions are only capable of making
Blacks insensitive to their humanity. No man or institution has
the power to destroy the basic humanity of Black people. The
reality of the humanity of Blacks is independent of racist attitudes and values. The humanity of Blacks is as certain as the
forces used by God to regulate the universe, as real as the principles that dominate life and death."[3]

So began the northern stream's search for historical roots that were
authentically Black, not imitational. This new quest carried some
back to the writings and sayings of Frederick Douglass, the great
abolitionist. For others the quest went beyond Frederick Douglass
to Nat Turner and Denmark Vesey, who led slave revolts.

These Black thinkers failed to realize that their disenchantment
with the civil-rights movement was due to their viewing southern
desegregation from a northern perspective. They were assuming
that desegregation was another way of facilitating "Negro" integration by means of imitation, which up to that time had been the
best-known northern strategy. But the southern leaders of the civil-
rights movement never thought of desegregation as a means of
becoming culturally White or losing their identity. Imitation had
no history in the South. The Blacks of the South wanted to desegre-
gate but remain culturally Black.

From Frederick Douglass (1817-95) the northern stream continued through W. E. B. DuBois (1868-1963), whose aim was to
consolidate Black America as a cultural nation, not through servi-
tude and menial labor as Booker T. Washington suggested, but on
the basis of education. DuBois saw that the Black nation could be
led by what he called the "talented tenth." In 1910 he founded the
Niagara Movement, which later became the NAACP. The idea of
the Black cultural nation stayed alive, but since education was still
beyond the reach of the masses of Black Americans, a different
basis for cultural nationalism was needed.

In the 1920s Marcus Garvey and the United Negro Improve-
ment Association (UNIA) attempted to consolidate the Black na-

tion around what most of us had in common, namely, Black religion. Instead of seeking a nationalism in America, he wanted to found a political nation in Africa. Before his back-to-Africa movement was sabotaged and Garvey deported, he managed to attract thousands of followers, especially in northeastern cities and particularly Harlem. With the Harlem Renaissance in the late 1920s and mid '30s, Blacks began to affirm in art, literature and music what Frederick Douglass, W. E. B. DuBois and Marcus Garvey had taught, namely, that our nonwhiteness is something to be proud of.

Patterned on the defunct Garvey movement came three Black religious sects, two of which were forms of Christianity-ism and one of which was Islam-ism. These were, respectively, the Peace Mission Movement, headed by Father Divine; the United House of Prayer for All People, headed by "Daddy" Grace; and the Nation of Islam, headed by Elijah Pool, who changed his name to Elijah Muhammad. All three were moderately successful.

Mr. Little
On May 19, 1925 in Omaha, Nebraska, a boy was born to the Reverend and Mrs. Earl Little, their fourth child. The Reverend Little, a Baptist preacher, was a dedicated organizer in the Garvey movement, often taking his son with him to his meetings of the UNIA. What little Mr. Little heard at those meetings made a profound impression on him. So did the violence which surrounded his family. When the KKK drove his family out of Omaha, they moved to Milwaukee, Wisconsin, and then to Lansing, Michigan—always followed by violence.

The Little's boy grew up to be one of the most influential Black leaders, a spokesman for the militant North, the inaugurator of the modern Black phase of our quest. His name was Malcolm.

Malcolm Little's formative years were disastrous. He was emotionally damaged, and his understanding of himself and his people was grossly distorted because he had given in to the assumptions of White racism. Malcolm later wrote that his father, in spite of his pro-Black philosophy,

was subconsciously so afflicted with the white man's brain-
washing of negroes that he inclined to favor the light ones, and
I was his lightest child. Most negro parents in those days would
almost instinctively treat any lighter children better than they
did the darker ones. It came directly from the slavery tradition
that the "mulatto," because he was visibly nearer to white, was
therefore "better." ...

   Out in the world later on, ... I was among the millions of
negroes who were insane enough to feel that it was some kind of
status symbol to be light-complexioned—that one was actually
fortunate to be born thus. But, still later, I learned to hate every
drop of white rapist's [his grandfather's] blood that is in me.[4]
After the murder of their father, the family was forced to go on wel-
fare, and Malcolm became involved in petty thefts around Lansing.
As his mother was slowly driven insane by the pressure of her
situation, the Little family fell apart. When Mrs. Little was institutionalized, Malcolm was taken from his home and placed in a series
of detention homes. During the summer of 1940 he visited his half-
sister, Ella, in Boston. There his eyes were opened to the oppression he had been subjected to in Lansing.

   Malcolm began to feel restless around White people, and his
White friends noticed it. He was a brilliant student, but when he
expressed a desire to be a lawyer, his eighth-grade teacher responded: "That's no realistic goal for a nigger." Instead, carpentry
was suggested as an appropriate career. Malcolm reflected,

   The more I thought afterwards about what he said, the more
   uneasy it made me. It just kept treading around in my mind. ...
   It was a surprising thing that I had never thought of it that way
   before, but I realized that whatever I wasn't, I was smarter than
   nearly all of those white kids. But apparently I was still not intelligent enough, in their eyes, to become whatever I wanted
   to be.
   It was then that I began to change—inside.[5]

Malcolm began to draw away from White people. It became a strain
even to sit in his eighth-grade classroom. "Where 'nigger' had

slipped off my back before, wherever I heard it now, I stopped and looked at whoever said it. And they looked surprised when I did."[6]

Like a time bomb, experiences like this would later explode.

Years of Deterioration From that time Malcolm began a general downhill slide which would take him back to Boston to live with his sister Ella, where he worked several odd jobs; through a two-year stay in Harlem, where his life took in drug abuse, hustling and assorted crimes; and back again to Boston, where he continued his life of crime. He was eventually busted on several counts of grand theft and sentenced to ten years in prison. Malcolm described himself at his lowest point in prison: "I preferred the solitary. . . . I would pace for hours like a caged leopard, viciously cursing aloud to myself. And my favorite targets were the Bible and God. But there was a legal limit to how much time one could be kept in solitary. Eventually, the men in the cellblock had a name for me: 'Satan.' Because of my antireligious attitude."

Malcolm Little's life changed direction in 1947 when he met fellow-inmate Bimbi, who made a strong impression on him. Bimbi's opinions on any given subject were highly respected, even by the prison guards. "Out of the blue one day, Bimbi told me flatly, as was his way, that I had some brains, if I'd use them. I had wanted his friendship, not that kind of advice. I might have cursed another convict, but nobody cursed Bimbi. He told me I should take advantage of the prison correspondence courses and the library."

Malcolm began to study English and penmanship through correspondence courses, and, after about a year, he could write a decent letter. "About then, too, influenced by having heard Bimbi often explain word derivations, I quietly started another correspondence course—in Latin."[7] Malcolm Little's life had turned decisively.

Undoing the Damage One day in 1948 Malcolm received a letter from his brother Philbert, who had been involved in a holiness church and had often told Malcolm that he and his church were praying for him. Only now the message was different. Philbert said that "he had discovered the 'natural religion for the black man,'. . .

something called 'the Nation of Islam.' "[8] A letter from his brother
Reginald instructed him not to eat any more pork or smoke any
more cigarettes. (Reginald also told Malcolm he'd show him how
to get out of prison. This struck a responsive chord.) Reginald
visited Malcolm and began to explain some of his new beliefs:

"Malcolm, if a man knew every imaginable thing that there is
to know, who would he be?"

"Well, he would have to be some kind of a god—"

Reginald said, "There's a *man* who knows everything."

"Who is that?"

"God is a man," Reginald said. "His real name is Allah."

Reginald went on. He said that God had 360 degrees of knowledge, . . . "the sum total of knowledge. . . . The devil has only
thirty-three degrees of knowledge—known as Masonry."

He told me that this God had come to America, and that he had
made himself known to a man named Elijah—"a black man, just
like us." This God had let Elijah know . . . that the devil's "time
was up."

"The devil is also a man," Reginald said.

"What do you mean?"

"The white man is the devil."

I never will forget: my mind was involuntarily flashing across
the entire spectrum of white people I had ever known. . . .

I said, "Without any exception?"

"Without any exception."[9]

Malcolm went on to think about all his encounters with White
people, and without exception they all were negative. The time
bomb was exploding! On a subsequent visit Reginald expounded
on what "white devils" had kept hidden from them. Concurring,
Malcolm was dramatically converted.

The truth can be quickly received . . . only by the sinner who
knows and admits that he is guilty of having sinned much.
Stated another way: only guilt admitted accepts truth. The Bible
again: the one people whom Jesus could not help were the Pharisees; they didn't feel they needed any help.

The very enormity of my previous life's guilt prepared me to accept the truth.

Not for weeks yet would I deal with the direct, personal application to myself, as a black man, of the truth. It still was like a blinding light.[10]

In an attempt to document Elijah Muhammad's teachings, Malcolm began an intensive program of self-education. His vocabulary increased by leaps and bounds as a result of his copying the whole dictionary by hand.

Why did Malcolm's brothers describe the Nation of Islam as the natural religion of the Black man? Elijah Muhammad had begun with his perceptions of the Black situation and had developed a mythology to explain it. According to this, the moon had been separated from the earth and then Allah created the first humans, a Black people who founded the Holy City of Mecca. Thirty per cent of this Black race was dissatisfied. Mr. Yacub, whose head was unusually large, began preaching dissatisfaction in Mecca and gained a large following. Eventually he and his 59,999 followers were exiled to the island of Patmos. Yacub became bitter toward Allah and decided as revenge to create a devil race.

He knew that the Black man contained two germs, black and brown, and that the brown germ was the morally weaker because it was lighter. Mr. Yacub died before completing his task, but he left rules for his followers by which brown people could marry only with other browns, and Blacks with Blacks. All Black babies were killed at birth, thereby assuring that the race would gradually grow lighter—first brown, then red, then yellow, then white. Because Whites were morally weakest, they were most susceptible to evil influence. They became a race of devils. When they eventually returned to the mainland, they began to turn the peaceful heaven on earth into a hell torn by quarreling and fighting.

Allah sent Moses to civilize the Whites, who would rule for six thousand years. Blacks would experience their devilishness firsthand through enslavement in America. But Allah did not forget his people: He sent Master W. D. Fard to tell Allah's message to Elijah

Muhammad, who would tell it to North America.[11] This bizarre mythological explanation of the origin of the White man was in part a reaction to White Christianity-ism's bizarre myths about the mark of Cain and the curse of Ham.

On his release from prison in the spring of 1952, Malcolm went to Detroit, where he became Malcolm X, a minister of Temple No. 1. From then until 1964 Malcolm X was the main exponent of Elijah Muhammad's doctrine. He built the Nation of Islam from the least successful into the most formidable of the post-Garvey religious movements. Malcolm's power of persuasion, his extensive knowledge of history, his remarkable ability to express complicated issues in simple parables, his wit and energy in organizing new temples, made the Nation of Islam one of the most powerful Black organizations in history.

Rearrangement
For twelve years Malcolm X had followed Elijah Muhammad and worked in the cause of the Black Muslim faith, becoming minister of the prestigious Temple No. 7 in Harlem. Then a rift began to develop between Malcolm and the Nation.

Los Angeles, July 3 [1963] (UPI)—Elijah Muhammad, 67-year-old leader of the Black Muslim movement, today faced paternity suits from two former secretaries who charged he fathered their four children.... Both women are in their twenties.... [They] charged they had intimacies with Elijah Muhammad from 1957 until this year. [One] alleged he fathered her two children and said she was expecting a third child by him ... [and] the other plaintiff said he was the father of her daughter.[12]

Hints of such problems had occurred as far back as 1955, but Malcolm had refused to believe them. At the same time Elijah Muhammad began to cut down Malcolm's character and work behind his back. Malcolm was suspended from the Nation for ninety days (December 2, 1963 to March 2, 1964) following a controversial statement made about the assassination of President Kennedy. He began to get reports that his death was being advocated by his closest associates. In his words, "My head felt like it was bleeding inside. I felt like my brain was damaged."[13]

Jettisoned Racism Finally, on March 8, 1964, when it appeared that his suspension would be indefinite, Malcolm called a news conference and announced his formal break with Elijah Muhammad and the Nation. From that time, Malcolm lived under the threat of assassination. He said, "Now, each day I live as if I am already dead."[14]

To gain a fresh perspective, Malcolm made a pilgrimage to Mecca, looking for answers to his questions about the Black situation. His experience there was profoundly enlightening, and led him into a prophetic role. He wrote his wife, Betty,

Never have I witnessed such sincere hospitality and the overwhelming spirit of true brotherhood as is practiced by people of all colors and races here in this Ancient Holy Land. . . . For the past week, I have been utterly speechless and spellbound by the graciousness I see displayed all around me by people *of all colors. . . .*

You may be shocked by these words from me. But on this pilgrimage, what I have seen, and experienced, has forced me to *re-arrange* much of my thought-patterns previously held, and to *toss aside* some of my previous conclusions. This was not too difficult for me. Despite my firm convictions, I have always been a man who tries to face facts, and to accept the reality of life as new experience and new knowledge unfolds it. I have always kept an open mind, which is necessary to the flexibility that must go hand in hand with every form of intelligent search for truth. . . .

I could see from this, that perhaps if white Americans could accept the Oneness of God, then perhaps, too, they could accept *in reality* the Oneness of Man—and cease to measure, and hinder, and harm others in terms of their "differences" in color. . . .

Never have I been so highly honored. Never have I been made to feel more humble and unworthy. Who would believe the blessings that have been heaped upon an *American Negro*?[15]

This was the final stage in the deprogramming of Malcolm X. Since he had swallowed the poisons of White racism, it may have taken the bitter medicine of Black racism to make him vomit the poison up. After a twelve-year dose, he was ready to see that humanity is not determined by race. It wasn't the teachings of Islam that opened his eyes. It was seeing, outside America, honest relationships among people of all colors. Here were human relations which had not been destroyed by the bigotry that had marked his life. He understood how the attitudes and motives of White people in America had affected Black people. "In my thirty-nine years on this earth, the Holy City had been the first time I had ever stood before the Creator of All and felt like a complete human being."[16] In one step he embraced the humanity of all people and jettisoned racism.

Living Manhood   After his return Malcolm X spoke in Chicago about his radical change of mind:

> In the past, I have permitted myself to be used to make sweeping indictments of all white people, and these generalizations have caused injuries to some white people who did not deserve them. Because of the spiritual rebirth which I was blessed to undergo as a result of my pilgrimage to the Holy City of Mecca, I no longer subscribe to sweeping indictments of one race. My pilgrimage ... served to convince me that perhaps American whites can be cured of the rampant racism which is consuming them and about to destroy this country. In the future, I intend to be careful not to sentence anyone who has not been proven guilty. I am not a racist and do not subscribe to any of the tenets of racism. In all honesty and sincerity it can be stated that I wish nothing but freedom, justice and equality: life, liberty and the pursuit of happiness—for all people.[17]

With his nonracist stance he began to re-evaluate other thoughts and values. His understanding of power and leadership opened up new dimensions.

> Mankind's history has proved from one era to another that the true criterion of leadership is spiritual. Men are attracted by

spirit. By power, men are *forced*. Love is engendered by spirit. By power, anxieties are created. . . .

I am in agreement one hundred per cent with those . . . who say that no government laws ever can *force* brotherhood. The only true world solution today is governments guided by true religion—of the spirit.[18]

Clearly his philosophy was changing, but to what? That we will never know. One thing is sure. The only way to account for Malcolm X's rise from the cesspool of society to become one of the most influential men in American history is the grace of God. Malcolm, having himself been humanized, gave us a new meaning to being Black: we were human. He liberated truths which had been locked up in the mythological doctrines of the Nation of Islam and delivered them to the smoldering victims of ghettoization.

Malcolm seems to have been a genuine seeker of truth, but the distortions of Christianity-ism prevented him from seeing the Bible as the real source of the truth about humanity. Malcolm X functioned as a prophet in enlightening us and condemning Christianity-ism with its view of Blacks—an enlightenment which used "borrowed capital"[19] from Christian truth but in the name of Islam. The challenge of Malcolm X forced the Black Christian to search the Scriptures for new insights about humanity. Although not realizing it, Malcolm X reoriented the Black collective consciousness toward a truer scriptural view of ourselves, opening our eyes to the image of God in us; he became the symbol and embodiment of that new consciousness.

In a way Malcolm was our humanity, as Ossie Davis said: "Malcolm was our manhood, our living, black manhood! This was his meaning to his people. And, in honoring him, we honor the best in ourselves. . . . He was and is—a prince—our black shining prince!"[20] Eldridge Cleaver wrote:

It was not the Black Muslim movement itself that was so irresistibly appealing to the true believers. It was the awakening into self-consciousness of twenty million Negroes which was so compelling. Malcolm X articulated their aspirations better than

any other man of our time. When he spoke under the banner of
Elijah Muhammad he was irresistible. When he spoke under his
own banner he was still irresistible. If he had become a Quaker,
a Catholic, or a Seventh-day Adventist, or a Sammy Davis-style
Jew, and if he had continued to give voice to the mute ambitions
in the black man's soul, his message would still have been triumphant: because what was great was not Malcolm X but the
truth he uttered.[21]

"Let's Cool It, Brothers"   As long as Malcolm X was speaking
under the banner of the Nation of Islam, he was not considered a
dangerous threat by the power elite. But when he founded the Organization of Afro-American Unity (OAAU) and began to speak
under his own banner, the threat increased. He began to affirm that
people are people regardless of color, that the issue is not Black versus White but oppressed versus oppressor, exploited versus ex-
ploiter; and the powerful feared he would eventually attract a
broad-based following with even international implications. His
intention to bring charges of human rights violations against this
country on the floor of the United Nations made him too much of a
threat. He had to be removed from the scene.

The OAAU needed a new program. A series of three public meetings was planned for the Audubon Ballroom (Harlem) to "arouse
interest," and Malcolm was to speak at each.

At the first meeting (January 24, 1965), Malcolm would trace the
roots of Black history from the great African civilizations through
slavery to the present. The second meeting (January 31) would con-
sist of Malcolm's discussion of the current Black situation and the
devices used to keep our people oppressed. At the third meeting
(February 7) Malcolm would reveal his long-awaited vision for
Black America and present the new OAAU program.

The January 24 and 31 meetings were held as planned. Because
of a conflict in Malcolm's schedule, however, the February 7 meeting had to be postponed to February 15. But early on the morning
of February 14 his home was fire-bombed while he, his wife and
four children were asleep. No one was hurt. Naturally, the February

15 meeting turned into a discussion of the bombing. The discussion of the new OAAU program and Malcolm's new vision was moved to the following Sunday, February 21. That day became the day to remember.[22]

"The people who entered the ballroom were not searched at the door. In recent weeks, Malcolm X had become irritable about this, saying, 'It makes people uncomfortable' and that it reminded him of Elijah Muhammad. 'If I can't be safe among my own kind, where can I be?' "

Malcolm arrived just before two o'clock. He said to a small group of his assistants that "he was going to state that he had been hasty to accuse the Black Muslims of bombing his home. 'Things have happened since that are bigger than what they can do. I know what they can do. Things have gone beyond that.... The way I feel, I ought not to go out there at all today,' Malcolm X said.... 'I'm going to ease some of this tension by telling the black man not to fight himself—that's all a part of the white man's big maneuver, to keep us fighting among ourselves, against each other. I'm not fighting anyone, that's not what we're here for.' "[23]

Malcolm could hear himself being introduced from the anteroom where he sat.

"And now, without further remarks, I present to you one who is willing to put himself on the line for you, a man who would give his life for you—I want you to hear, listen, to understand—one who is a trojan for the black man!"

There was applause, and he walked out, smiling and nodding. The applause diminished.

Then the familiar ringing greeting, "*Asalaikum*, brothers and sisters!"

"Asalaikum salaam!" some in the audience responded.

About eight rows of seats from the front, then, a disturbance occurred. In a sudden scuffling, a man's voice was raised angrily, "Take your hand out of my pocket!" The entire audience was swiveling to look. "Hold it! Hold it! Don't get excited," Malcolm X said crisply. "Let's cool it, brothers—"[24]

One woman said it looked like a firing squad.

A Flash in the Pan

Along with the OAAU, Malcolm X had founded Muslim Mosque, Incorporated. He intended these to function in the Black movement as a political (secular) arm and a religious arm respectively. Consequently those who tried to carry on Malcolm's work after his assassination, did so according to these two perspectives.

The Black Phase: A Secular Approach   Those who tried the secular approach well remembered when Malcolm said:

> No religion will ever make me forget the condition of our people in this country. No religion will ever make me forget the continued fighting with dogs against our people in this country. No religion will make me forget the police clubs that come up 'side our heads. No God, no religion, no thing will make me forget it until it stops, until it's finished, until it's eliminated.

> Although I'm still a Muslim, . . . I'm not here to try and change your religion. I'm not here to argue or discuss anything that we differ about, because it's time for us to submerge our differences and realize that it is best for us to first see that we have the same problem, a common problem—a problem that will make you catch hell whether you're a Baptist or a Methodist, or a Muslim or a nationalist. . . . You're going to catch hell just like I am. We're all in the same boat and we all are going to catch the same hell.[25]

> If I discover that I am caught up in a religion that will not allow me to fight the battle for black men, then I say to hell with that religion![26]

Black people would need to forget about differences if they were to combat racism. Malcolm called this "the Gospel of Black Nationalism." It was to transcend all groups, churches and clubs in the Black community in the same way the gospel of Christ that Billy Graham preached transcended denominations. He encouraged his followers to "join any organization that has a gospel that's for the uplifting of the Black man."[27]

Many remembered the scathing indictments Malcolm made about "Christianity" during his days in the Nation of Islam. They also remembered the hostility between him and the Nation after his break with Elijah Muhammad. Those who had been attracted to Malcolm but not to Islam carried on with an anti-religious bias in general and an anti-Christian bias in particular. What started out as an open-minded approach, however, quickly turned into secular humanism. The Black secularists, holding no truth as absolute, hoped to see all the variant elements of our culture merge into

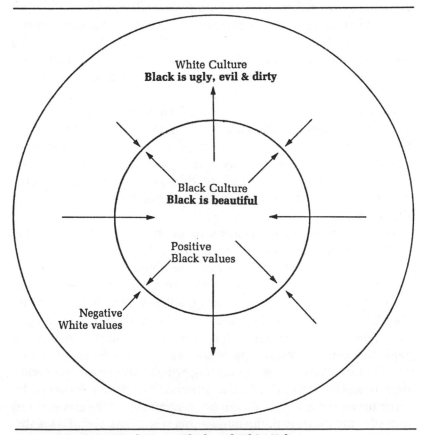

Figure 6: Confrontation between Black and White Values.

agreement and unity through a process of gradual synthesis. A religiously neutral Black culture would emerge, a unified whole, excluding the Black church.

Black Awareness   Nothing short of a cultural revolution resulted as these ideas trickled down to the folks on the street. For the first time we chose our own term by which to be known: that term was *Black,* and we tried to consolidate around it. Like the principle alluded to in 1 Corinthians 1:27-28, we took the word *(Black)* which was most despised in melting pot culture and confounded America as we redefined it to be a term of dignity.

Whether we knew it or not, the choice of the term *Black* was a very clever one. As an ideal in Black culture, Black was beautiful by definition. As a concept in the larger, White-oriented culture, Black was ugly, evil and dirty. This set up an immediate and continuous confrontation in the minds of those who adopted the term *Black,* a confrontation between our new-found positive view of Blackness and the traditional value system's negative view (figure 6). It had two effects, especially on the youth of Black America. First,it radicalized the urban masses. Thus we suddenly had a vast army of militant-minded people ready to be led by new Black leadership—a vast army also open to manipulation in the name of Blackness.

Among the alienated victims of ghettoization, however, the value confrontation had a second effect: it heaped frustration on frustration. Their expectations had been heightened by the social upheaval of the '60s. Yet they had experienced no real benefit from either the civil-rights movement or the Black movement. To them, the only alternative was to strike out and vent their pent-up anger.

For the first time in our history, the hostility and suspicion we generally perpetuated among ourselves was now focused outside —at White society and at the White-owned businesses in our communities. The Watts riot in the summer of '65 was followed by other urban riots in '65, '66 and '67. Amazingly, in the passion and heat of these early riots, the businesses which had "Soul Brother" on their windows were untouched by the destruction. The assassination of Martin Luther King, Jr., in April of 1968 triggered another wave of riots. The hundred years of hatred poured into the Black community was suddenly regurgitated, and America for the first time felt its effect and was shocked.

Many of the newly radicalized militants believed that freedom and dignity were within our grasp. According to the new consensus, to assert one's Blackness was to demonstrate that one had achieved the goals of the historic Black quest. We soon discovered, however, that mere assertiveness could not bear the freight of our whole humanity.

Though we did not achieve the fullness of freedom and dignity, we learned several things from Black awareness. We learned, for instance, that we have human dignity, as we are, in our non-Whiteness. We also learned that the Black community has characteristics as a nation, that our culture and consciousness are worth affirming and preserving. Finally, we learned that racism, like sin, has been institutionalized in American society at all levels and in every area of life.

Black Power Among us were those who thought our people

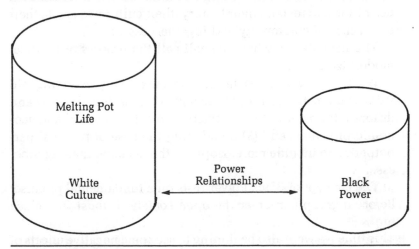

Figure 7: Black Power.

would find freedom and dignity when they organized and consolidated their political, economic and social power into a unified force. The exercise of power by Black people was thought to be the key. This became known as Black Power. Though Malcolm X was the real father of this movement and Marcus Garvey coined the phrase *Black Power*, it was Stokely Carmichael who made it popular.

Those in the Black Power movement advocated five things: (1) that we deal with the melting pot system not on a moral base, but on a power base from a position of strength (because by this time White America was considered amoral); (2) that we form coalitions with other groups only at points of agreement and not as allies; (3) that we maintain control in our own Black communities—economically, politically and socially; (4) that we develop a Black melting pot; and (5) that we form new institutions to express the new realities of a Black-conscious people (figure 7). As Stokely Carmichael and Charles Hamilton wrote:

> Black people must redefine themselves, and only *they* can do that. Throughout this country, vast segments of the black communities are beginning to recognize the need to assert their own definitions, to reclaim their history, their culture; to create their own sense of community and togetherness. . . .
>
> The next step is what we shall call the process of political modernization. . . .
>
> We mean by it three major concepts: (1) questioning old values and institutions of the society; (2) searching for new and different forms of political structure to solve political and economic problems; and (3) broadening the base of political participation to include more people in the decision-making process. . . .
>
> The concept of Black Power rests on a fundamental premise: *Before a group can enter the open society, it must first close ranks.*[28]

By this time we were also beginning to see some negative effects of our own unrighteousness. Ironically, the closer we came to our

goal of overthrowing White oppression, the more our own ungodliness surfaced to oppress us. Negro pimps were now Black pimps,
and Negro dope pushers were now Black dope pushers. In the
words of the Last Poets, "Niggers change into doing 'Black' nigger
things."[29]

Ethical content could have saved the Black Power movement.
But the leaders had already swallowed secular humanism. Thus all
moral decisions were left up to the individual. The movement was
drowned by do-your-own-thing-ism. We fell short of true freedom
and human dignity as our own ungodliness began to hold us back.
This shouldn't have surprised us, since this is the natural effect
unrighteousness has on all people and all nations.

The Black Power movement gave us some other valuable insights, however. It showed that it is necessary to demonstrate the
beauty of being Black through a corporate model (body life). It also
taught us that Black Power alone could not guarantee that we would
not substitute the rule of "a hateful honky for a nasty nigger."[30]
And finally, we saw that Black economic power at best would still
be tied up with the American economic system.

Black Revolutionism Many of us believed that the American
system was still having a negative effect on the Black nation, in
spite of Black power. Many thought that we were on the right track
in looking for freedom and dignity within ourselves, but the trick
was to remove the overwhelming influence which was preventing
"us" from being "us." The American system had to be replaced:
Enter the Black revolution. The revolutionaries weren't concerned
about what would happen after the revolution because optimism
was still strong; we would "cross that bridge" when we got there.
After the revolution everything would be reversed. Black folks
would be on top, and the melting pot folks would feel the flames
for a change while they followed Booker T. Washington's advice,
earning a place in the new order.

Though Christianity was condemned as being too otherworldly
and naive, Black revolutionism resembled early Black theology in
its structural model (figure 8). The river Jordan, which had meant

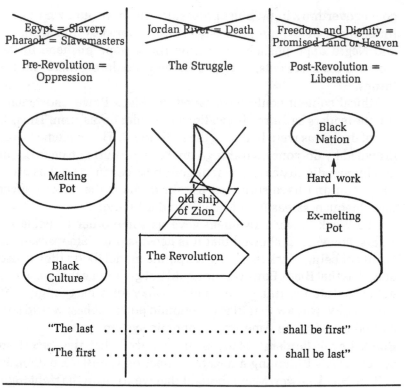

Figure 8: Black Revolutionism Compared to Historic Black Theology.

death, was replaced by the *struggle*. On this side of the struggle we were oppressed. On the other side we would be liberated, along with our oppressed brothers and sisters; we would be first among the cultural nations. In Black revolutionism the main question was not, What are you going to do when the judgment comes? but, What are you going to do when the *revolution* comes? Instead of the Garden of Eden, they harked back to an idyllic life in Mother Africa. A heroic but dead Malcolm took the place of the living Jesus. Fred Hampton, Mark Clark, the New York Twenty One, Huey Newton and others were substituted for the persecuted saints and the martyrs. And the ideal society after the revolution was substituted for heaven. For all of the fuss about the naiveté of early Black theology, some of the revolutionaries turned out to be far more naive; the revolution they were talking about was just as impossible as overthrowing the slave system. Only this time the impossibility was in ourselves. Theologian William E. Pannell beautifully summed up this impossibility in a conversation with me in 1972. When I asked him if he thought there would be a revolution he said, "No, because the revolution can't get past Saturday night!"

Malcolm X, as far back as May 1964, recognized this inertia when he said, "Nowadays, as our people begin to wake up, they're going to realize, they've been *talking* about ... revolution. You can't talk that stuff to me unless you're really for one. I don't even want to hear it unless you're really for one. And most [of] you *aren't*. When the deal goes down, [you'll] back out."[31]

The revolution turned out to be only a "flash in the pan." Many of those who had been involved in the quest for freedom and dignity dropped out. They concluded that the goals of the revolution were unattainable, so they settled for fulfilling some limited personal goals. Why didn't the revolution materialize? Partly because *liberation* as a goal of the revolution had never been defined. Under humanism, the definition of liberation was left up to the individual. For example, a "brother" might consider himself "liberated" when he was able to shack up with his girlfriend without the disapproval of his peers. Once he had achieved his personal goal, he would drop out of the revolutionary cause. Definitions of liberation not drawn from the Word of God will always fall short of true liberation. By leaving the definition up to the humanistic revolutionaries, the failure of the revolution was assured.

When the revolution failed to materialize, however, it was more than a missed shot at progress. It was a step backward. As would-be revolutionaries dropped out of the cause to do their own thing, they killed the possibility of a new Black unity. The massive dropout rate produced a huge number of contradictory do-your-own-thing-isms.

The early optimistic thinkers had not anticipated this because

they did not have a biblical understanding of sin's effect on a
people. Achieving justice required a total radical change in us as
well as in our environment. We could not have a revolution without divine help. We found out that the failure of White humanism
showed up in Black humanism too, and this failure meant falling
short of our revolutionary goal because of unrighteousness (Rom
3:23).

Salvage Attempts Some people tried to stop the mass exodus
from the quest by trying to salvage the dead revolution. I call these
people Neo-Black revolutionaries. Basically, they equated revolution with mere change and said, "Since we have had a *change* in
Black consciousness, we have had a revolution." This linguistic
sleight of hand did not fool many. It only served as further justification for pursuing counter-revolutionary, personal goals.

The erosion of Neo-Black revolutionism wiped out almost all the
remnant still in the "quest." Those few left embraced Pan-Africanism. Ironically, the Pan-African idea originated with the Black
church. Under the banner of Pan-Africanism, the thirteenth and
fourteenth episcopal districts of the African Methodist Episcopal
Church were formed in west and south Africa.[32] In it the oneness of
all people of African descent was affirmed. By now the Pan-Africanism had been secularized and infused with Marxist ideology.
For Black America, secular Pan-Africanism was too little too late. It
never became a consensus. However, the movement reminded us
that we as a people have an important role to play among other
African peoples and as part of the Third World.

A Secular Gamble The disintegrated condition of the Black
movement today is a testimony to the inadequacy of secularism. As
early as 1968 its inadequacy was becoming visible to thinkers.
Black unity, which had been the basis of all the optimism, was on
the verge of collapse. Secularism was beginning to show its self-
destructive nature.

Although the Black movement had long disqualified the historic Black church and accused its theology of being invalid, its
theological dynamic survived remarkably the torrents of criticism

which came from the militants. Indeed the theological dynamic still had a powerful influence on Black consciousness. This dynamic was so resilient that even Nikki Giovanni, a leading poet of secularism and de-Christianization, could not by-pass it.

The title of her first album, *Truth Is on Its Way*, expressed the prevailing Black sentiment that we did not yet have the truth but somehow we would succeed in finding and consolidating it.[33] Giovanni needed a medium which would capture her verbal power and intensify her ability to preach her message of Black secularism. She chose one of the most powerful elements of Black culture—gospel music. (Ironically, the new militants had considered gospel music, a part of the oral tradition of the Black church, to be an expression of the White man's religion.)

To lead off *Truth Is on Its Way*, Nikki Giovanni juxtaposed "Peace, Be Still" with her poem "The Great Pax Whitie." Here was gospel music, the very fruit of the Black church, being used for its spiritual and cultural power. For Nikki Giovanni, gospel music functioned merely as a preamble for her secular ideology, which was based on the view that Christianity was the very core of the White man's past atrocities.

This use of gospel music was not a phenomenon restricted to Giovanni. It was indicative of what was going on among Black thinkers in general. During the late '60s and early '70s it became apparent that absolute secularism was faltering. Secular humanism would never dislodge the Black church as a base, even though the church had up to that time been left out of the Black movement. Across the country, militants were reluctantly conceding to the church a minor role in the movement. We now saw during Black week on many campuses the Black church being given a piece of the action.

In using the oral tradition of the church, the new Black thinkers were taking a gamble. Would Black unity have the desired secular character or a Christian one? Secularists had no choice. Their only hope lay in a synthesis between secularism and the Black church (figure 9). Humanism needed some theological "propping

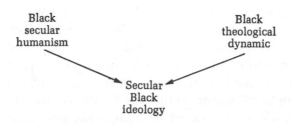

Figure 9: Proposed Black Ideology.

up on its leaning side."

These days saw the emergence of new Black theologians like Albert Cleage. For many of them the ultimate reference point was the Black experience itself, not the Word of God. Even Huey P. Newton, leader of the Black Panther Party, which at the time was still in the para-military phase of its development, was beginning to talk about returning to the church. But this new Black theology was largely ignored by the Black church, which since then has hardly budged from its traditional stance.

So the '70s witnessed the results of Black ungodliness. Secularism succeeded only in producing cultural confusion. Black humanism degenerated into do-your-own-thing-ism, and that in turn has led to libertarianism (looking-out-for-number-one-ism) and hedonism (if-it-feels-good-do-it-ism). There is even a new Black bourgeoisie-ism (materialism), hanging on to the same false values we used to condemn in White society. Although some left-over splinter groups remain, trying to re-establish the momentum of the militant Black movement, the dynamic and the cultural consensus of the '60s is gone (figure 10).

Layers of Religion

The Black church did lose some of its pre-Black movement influence, but it has by and large survived in relative health and has even made a significant comeback. With the disintegration of Black humanism, the remainder of the Black movement was in danger of

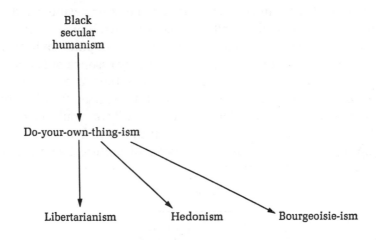

Figure 10: Degeneration of Black Ideology.

reversing its secular development. Many thought the movement was drifting back in the unthinkable direction of the church. For the militants, if a non-Christian ethnic identity was going to be developed, they would have to find another crutch to buttress Black humanism.

The Post-Black Phase: A Religious Approach For many who tried a religious approach to liberation, the alternative by the early to mid '70s became Islam. The Nation of Islam had been with us through the '60s, but the new Black militants did not take it too seriously because of their commitment to secularism. However, with the deterioration of secularism, they were now taking a hard second look.

They perhaps began to remember when Malcolm said, "I am and always will be a Muslim. My religion is Islam. . . . I am going to organize and head a new mosque in New York City, known as Muslim Mosque, Inc. This gives us a religious base and the spiritual force necessary to rid our people of the vices that destroy the moral fiber of our community."[34]

Through Islam they hoped to salvage and revitalize the ailing

dream of a de-Christianized Black culture. They also wanted to develop a Black Islamic theological dynamic. This, however, posed
some serious problems because, contrary to the popular myth that
it is the religion of our African roots, the very essence of Islam is
rooted in a language and culture which is neither Afro-American
nor African, but Arab. Thus Islam cannot take on itself the identity
of any non-Arab culture. Islam and Black culture would have to
function in an "oil and water" relationship, the oil layer of supraculture being Islam and the water layer of culture being Black
humanism. They never blend.

Islam

Black Humanism

The new Black Muslims eventually wanted to replace this unstable
dualism with a solid theological and cultural unity. Some tried.
But to do this, they either had to absolutize Islam, thereby wiping
out secularism, or absolutize secularism, thereby wiping out Islam.
Neither method brought success.

Because of its exclusively Arab orientation, Islam as a religious
motif fails because it cannot foster the desired cohesion in Black
culture. Islam's adherents have tended to develop not an appreciation for legitimate Black culture, but a disdain and suspicion of it.
Yet they have thus far been unable to escape Black culture. Many of
them still speak Black English and still like jazz; and in Islam you
can neither worship Allah with jazz nor pray to him in Black
English.

Those who advocate Islam seem to forget that wherever Islam
has historically spread beyond its original geo-ethnic cradle (the
Arabian peninsula) to become the absolute religion, it spread primarily by the sword. "There is no God but Allah and Mohammed
is his prophet. Either submit to him or die." Needless to say, this
meant the rupture of the non-Arab culture and usually its replacement by the Arab Islamic culture. In Africa, where the spread of
Islam was not accompanied by total cultural rupture and replace-

ment, Islam has become merely an oil layer over the water layer of a native belief system.

Among Black Americans, the new Islamic believers have chosen an evangelistic strategy for the spread of Islam. They know that the rupture and replacement strategy will be counterproductive, to say the least. Besides, it would be logistically impossible. So through evangelism they have produced an "oil and water" cultural dualism, just as in Africa.

Islam

Native Belief System

An Islamic Dynamic?   Some of these Islamic thinkers have seen this dualistic folly and have followed the approach of Wallace D. Muhammad, son of Elijah Muhammad and leader of American Muslim Mission. Mr. Muhammad may have seen that absolute Islam was beginning to falter and that Islam would never dislodge the Black church. He began in the late '70s reluctantly to concede to the Black church a minor role as part of a general Black belief system. He was moving toward a Black synthesis, a far cry from his father's position.

The late Elijah Muhammad had looked at White Christianity-ism and built its mirror image, a Black Islam-ism. What Elijah Muhammad saw was a White man's religion, a Christian heresy which denied that it had anything to do with the *physical* world. What he created was a Black man's religion, an Islamic heresy which denied that it had anything to do with the *spiritual* world. As we have seen, the substance of the White Christianity-ism was a set of unbiblical myths which had justified the oppression of the Black man in America. As we have also seen, the substance of the Nation of Islam was a set of non-Qur'ānic myths which justified our total separation (by choice) from White society and the establishment of our own Islamic state in America.

When Wallace Muhammad inherited the reins of leadership after his father's death, he inaugurated sweeping changes in the life and racial policy of the sect, signified by its name changes.[35] Many in the Black church were pleasantly shocked when the Muslims went from being belligerent to being gracious toward them. In his view, neither the theology of the Black church (expressed in oral tradition) nor the beliefs of the Nation of Islam (expressed in doctrinaire ideology) were key to understanding Black history or culture; rather both were merely products of our history and culture. As such they could merge. This is why, at Mosque No. 2 in Chicago, gospel choirs have been invited to sing some of their songs after the Islamic services. Mr. Muhammad knows that if Islam is to be successful among Blacks, then it will need cultural "propping up on the leaning side." This combination is the only hope the Islamic believers now have to establish a place in the Black cultural fabric. By appealing to this proposed general belief system, Muslims have attempted to win our people to Islam.

Brother Muhammad appears to have solved the oil and water problem, but a difficulty remains. A syncretism of Christianity and Islam can never be true to both. It will either be primarily Christian in form and belief or primarily Islamic. To ensure that the combination does not become predominantly Christian, Mr. Muhammad has added a further layer of Islamic doctrine, which has only served to reintroduce the oil and water problem.

Another problem remains as well. According to the principle of the economy of thought, why make things more complicated than they have to be? In other words, why bother with this cumbersome combination or this irrelevant Islamic supraculture at all? We have done fine without them, so who needs them now? The soul dynamic has carried us and inspired our people thus far.

This is a question asked not by skeptics but by the Black church itself. It is a question which has already been answered by the church in its oral tradition. Someone has said:

We've come this far by faith
  leaning on the Lord,
  trusting in his Holy Word.
He's never failed me yet.

Oh, Oh, Oh . . . can't turn around.
We've come this far by faith.
And another:
As long as I've got King Jesus
I don't need nobody else!
If oil and water won't blend, then clearly the Black movement is at a
crossroads.

Post-Black Blues

The original goals of the post-Malcolm Black movement were the
liberation of the Black community from oppression and exploitation, and the development of a new Black culture that pulled together all its diverse elements. Sadly, both goals have been lost in
the dualistic sauce. The de-Christianization of the Black movement
was supposed to be an essential part of the first goal. However, with
secularization came do-your-own-thing-ism. The result of Islami-
zation has thus far been legalism and a preoccupation with works
righteousness (that fifty-one per cent which would tip the scale to
enter paradise).

Gone are social concern and activism on behalf of the poor and
oppressed. Gone is the ethical "oughtness" for this concern and
activism. Gone is the cultural unity which many assumed was
achievable. Gone, in short, is all warrant for the optimism of the
midsixties. Black secularism and Islam, whether one is absolutized or both juxtaposed in an unwanted dualism, have gutted the
very soul of the militant Black movement. The goals of the Black
movement have been betrayed, and now the hope of developing a
positive Black ethnicity is on the critical list.

Thus far the historic Black church has produced the only unified soul dynamic in the Black community. In fact, history shows
us that no Black movement has survived for long apart from the
church and its theological dynamic. The secular and Islamic Black
intellectuals have failed to produce it, and no cultural identity is
possible without it. A de-Christianized Black culture will always
lack theological and cultural unity. Black people will simply never

achieve this unity without the Black church. Yet, for some, the Black church is still Christianity, and Christianity is still the White man's religion. This, then, is the new Black crisis. This is why many today have the Post-Black blues.

Becoming   The Black militants who pronounced the death of the civil-rights movement never saw that the theological dynamic was an application of the scriptural message and not an extension of White Christianity-ism. The doctrine of White supremacy (a fruit of European philosophy) had never infected Black theology. Not seeing this, the militant Black thinkers rejected the theological dynamic and with it the power of God's Word. This is why the Black secular approach and the Post-Black religious approach failed.

About Malcolm X, however, there was nothing static. In the end he was in a state of flux. But what was Brother Malcolm heading toward? In January 1965 he confessed to Alex Haley, "The so-called 'moderate' civil rights organizations regard me as 'too militant' and the so-called 'militant' organizations avoid me as 'too moderate.' *They won't let me turn the corner.*"[36] Even Malcolm himself could not yet define this philosophical corner. On the Thursday before he died he told a reporter, "I can't put my finger on exactly what my philosophy is now, but I am flexible."[37]

For this reason many of the new militants turned their backs on Brother Malcolm. They began to openly criticize him for being too "confused to be seriously followed any longer." The word in Harlem was that "he doesn't know what he believes in." Some even accused him of being all talk, a con man, while Dr. Martin Luther King and others were getting "beat over the head" for the cause.[38]

But Malcolm simply pursued truth and freedom for our people wherever they led. Those who harshly criticized him for his new flexibility only revealed their shortsightedness. They did not understand the real significance of Brother Malcolm.

Some have suggested that Malcolm was headed in a biblical direction. If this is true and if the integrity he showed in the pursuit of truth was what it appears to have been, then surely on his arrival he would have acknowledged the Lord of the Scriptures as being "Lord of all." But given the mood of the Black community and the sorry condition of Christianity at that time, if he had arrived at this conclusion I wonder if those who followed him would still have accepted and respected him? Would he have been rejected as a prophet and branded a traitor by those who still confused Christianity with White Christianity-ism?

Only God knows the answers to the riddle of Malcolm X, and it is with God alone that our questions should rest. Those who have tried to extrapolate the direction of his life to a particular ideological, philosophical or religious destination have, in my judgment, missed the mark.

Furthermore, the issue of his destination is not what was important and valuable in his life. We lost him while he was in a state of "becoming," and it was the becoming itself that made Malcolm X "our living Black manhood." True humanity is to be in a perpetual state of becoming. This manifestation of becoming, like the ongoing quest for freedom and dignity, was what made the contribution of Malcolm X so valuable to our historic quest, and we can be thankful for it.

Chapter 9

A Great
Legacy

W HEN PAUL SPOKE to the intellectuals of Athens he used a remarkable poetic quotation from Epimenides, a sixth-century B.C. Cretan poet (Acts 17:23, 27-28). In Titus 1:12 Paul again quotes from Epimenides, calling him a prophet. I'd call him a cultural prophet. The Bible thus indicates that all nations, including the Black nation, may have had cultural prophets. Whether they are Christian is not necessarily the issue. Since God is Lord of all, the real issue is whether they were witnesses to God's Word in what they did and said.

Stereo Viewpoint
As we have seen, the southern quest for freedom and dignity

started with the Colored phase and has gone through the Neo-Colored and Neo-Negro phases. This southern stream has generally been oriented to church culture.

The northern quest started with the Negro phase and has gone through Black awareness, Black power and Black revolutionism. This northern stream has generally been oriented to nonchurch culture.

Of course, the two streams overlapped and benefited from each other. Put together, what we learned from them is similar to some things the Old Testament teaches. Let's now look at these streams in stereo.

From the southern stream we learned the following:

1. Racism is deeper than slavery or segregation. The end of slavery was not the beginning of freedom and dignity for our people. Slavery, though an expression of racism, was not the total picture of racism. The absence of slavery saw racism re-emerge in Jim-Crowism, segregation, disenfranchisement and exploitive economics. Even when segregation was defeated by the law of the land, racism itself was not erased because segregation is not the total picture of racism either. Racism survived in the hearts of many, ready to be applied in new ways. The survival of racism reveals the farce of White humanism, since racism is a form of oppression and oppression is a form of human unrighteousness.

2. The melting pot is not the answer. Integration, though a fruit of liberation, is not the total picture of liberation. While it is preferable to have access to the melting pot lifestyle rather than to be excluded from it, entrance is not worth being stripped of our cultural identity. True integration should never mean assimilation; the melting pot system is unable to produce freedom and dignity for Black people.

3. The Bible is our basis for freedom and dignity. The parallels between Hebrew history and Black history reveal that life cannot be lived only on an otherworldly basis. Freedom and dignity for our people, like the promised land for the Hebrews, has as much to do with this life as with the next. The theological dynamic which

emerged from the message of the Bible can give us wisdom to see through the phony nature of White Christianity-ism as we embrace and apply the truths of Christianity.

4. We must develop the resources we already have and unite around them. This is essential if we are going to achieve the goals of our quest. The soul dynamic is one such resource, and we can be proud of it. When applied properly, it can have a profound effect on Black people and on America at large.

From the northern stream we learned the following:

1. White humanism is bankrupt, and any Black strategy which depends on it is doomed to fail. When we tried to be acceptable to White society by imitating the melting pot lifestyle, for example, we only gave in to White standards and imitated White racism. Besides, our ability to imitate White folks was still unacceptable because we were still Black. The result of this was complexion consciousness, self-hatred, feelings of inferiority, and economic stress among our people. The only ones who seemed to have succeeded were those who "passed" for White, but they lived their lives in bondage to a lie. Any strategy based on genetics and environment is unworkable and reinforces oppression.

2. There is dignity in Black humanness and beauty in Black culture. Our culture and consciousness, therefore, are worth affirming and preserving. The best way to do this is through "body life" —an active, caring concern for each other, especially for those who suffer most from oppression. Without body life there is no guarantee that Black power will not just end up substituting a "hateful honky for a nasty nigger."

3. We need a radical change if we want justice. Such a change must be revolutionary, transforming us and our environment. This is impossible without God's help. Without God's truth and power at the root of our quest for justice, we are left with Black humanism; and Black humanism is guaranteed to fail because of Black unrighteousness.

4. If our community functions as a nation, we can move toward freedom and dignity. But successfully dealing with racism on an

individual basis will prove impossible because, like sin, racism is institutionalized in American society. Functioning as a cultural nation will help equip us to deal with racism from a position of strength. We need to control the politics of our community and, where appropriate, make coalitions with other groups at points of agreement—but not as allies. We also need to control the economics of our community. But we must remember that, while Black economic power is important, it is not the final solution because, ultimately, it is tied up with the American economic system. In short, we need new institutions on which to build a new cultural nationalism. We have an important role to play among other African and Third World peoples, and functioning as a nation will help us fulfill that role.

Prophets in Parallel

Dr. Martin Luther King, Jr., was the culminating cultural prophet of the southern stream, while Malcolm X was the culminating cultural prophet of the northern stream. The perspectives of these two prophets, from a humanistic standpoint, apparently contradict each other. But a God-centered perspective shows a complementary relationship between the two. The relationship between the contributions of these two men has been one of the greatest riddles in Black history. Part of the problem has arisen from a failure to see them in terms of the northern stream/southern stream mode.

Let's take a look at these two prophets in parallel.

1. Martin was a prophet from the South; Malcolm was a prophet from the North.

2. Martin exposed the sin of omission (what they *did not* do) of American Bible-believing Christianity; Malcolm exposed the sin of commission (what they did do—racism) of American Christianity-ism.

3. Martin exposed relational racism; Malcolm exposed institutional racism.

4. Martin was against segregation; Malcolm was against our losing Black identity through phony integration.

5. Martin advocated gracious love; Malcolm advocated raw truth.

6. Martin worked for moral and spiritual power; Malcolm worked for political and economic power.

7. Martin was a prophet for nonviolence, the southern strategy; Malcolm was a prophet of militancy, the northern strategy.

8. Martin came from a Black church, and church-oriented people followed him because he provided recognizable leadership as he called America to repent; Malcolm came from the streets, and street people followed him because he crystallized and articulated their hurts as he exposed systematic oppression.

9. When Martin went North to Chicago, Illinois, to improve the economic condition of the masses trapped in the ghetto, his strategy had little success; when Malcolm went South to address the participants in the Selma-to-Montgomery march, his strategy was less acceptable to the leaders of the march.

10. Toward the end of his life Martin began moving toward a more militant position; toward the end of his life Malcolm began moving toward a more conciliatory position.

11. Martin expressed the theological side of soul dynamic; Malcolm expressed the cultural side of soul dynamic.

12. Martin predicted his death shortly before it happened; so did Malcolm.

13. Martin had a vision of a great opportunity for our people but was assassinated before he was able to articulate it; Malcolm experienced the same fate.

14. Martin died at age thirty-nine; so did Malcolm.

Both Martin's and Malcolm's lives were parallel, in a sense, to Moses' life; they brought us to the brink of an opportunity, but they never entered it. What opportunity did they see? The answer to that question could be the key to why God in his sovereignty brought us forth as a cultural nation out of the horrors of slavery.

Kingdoms and Streams

One of the clearest notions in the soul dynamic is the idea that we are in this land for a special purpose. Since the deaths of Malcolm and Martin we have balked at the river Jordan, and we are once again wandering in circles. Perhaps looking at the biblical kingdom of Israel at a later stage in its history can shed new light on our situation.

Israel had divided into a southern kingdom and a northern kingdom. The southern kingdom stayed within the pattern of Yahwism, the true worship of God, but it became an empty tradition. The result of their indifference was the Babylonian conquest. The northern kingdom tried to replace Yahwism with paganism. The result was instability, apostasy, splintering, violent disputes between northern factions, assassinations, the Assyrian conquest and, finally, obliteration.

In the historic Black quest the southern stream stayed within the pattern of the church, but it has become a formal tradition. The result has been indifference toward God and the loss of the prophetic power we had discovered in the civil-rights movement. The northern stream tried to replace the theological dynamic with an alien religious base (Islam, secularism and the like). The result has been instability, apostasy, splintering, violent disputes between northern factions, assassinations, and the loss of Black culture as a unified force.

We can thank the southern stream for showing us that freedom and dignity are not found in the melting pot. We can thank the northern stream for showing us that freedom and dignity are not found within ourselves.

The Law and the "Quest"

If we look at how God used the law in the Old Testament to disciple the people of Israel, we may find further parallels with the Black experience to instruct us.

Paul asks, "What, then, was the purpose of the law? It was added *because of transgressions* until the Seed to whom the promise referred had come" (Gal 3:19). The Israelites' ordeal of slavery and their consequent social problems were going to keep them from surviving as a nation—and keep them from receiving the promised Seed (Christ). Without the law they would never have survived to fulfill their destiny as the nation through whom the Messiah of the world would come.

What then is the purpose of the soul dynamic? It was added *because of transgressions* until the Joshua phase should come in which our destiny would be fulfilled. The Black nation's ordeal of slavery and its consequent social problems would have kept us from surviving to see the Joshua phase. Without the soul dynamic we would never fulfill our destiny as a cultural nation.

What was the function of the law? "The law was our *schoolmaster* to bring us unto Christ" (Gal 3:24 KJV). Through the law Israel learned about the One whom God would send and what God was going to do through their people.

What was the comparable function of our "inheritance," the knowledge we gained from the phases of our quest? The inheritance was our *schoolmaster* to bring us to the Joshua phase. Through our inheritance we learned much about the Joshua phase and what it can do through us.

What was the result of the law? "We know that whatever the law says, it says to those who are under the law, *so that every mouth may be silenced* and ... [that] no living man can be beyond the judgment of God" (Rom 3:19). "Indeed it is the straight-edge of the Law that shows us how crooked we are" (Rom 3:20 Phillips). Failure to keep the law made Israel shut up when they began to brag about their own righteousness before God.

What was the result of our quest for liberation? Whatever the quest means, it communicates to those who are aware *so that every mouth may be silenced*. Indeed, it is the high ideal of liberation that shows us how *unliberated* we are! The failure, for example, of the Black revolution illustrates the effect of sin.

Scripture describes sin as "missing the mark," or "falling short." Understanding how our sin and ungodliness affect us in our pursuit of freedom and dignity can be key to understanding the significance and necessity of a Joshua phase. We have in our Black heritage a great legacy, and we should be proud of it. But it has only given us a glimpse of our potential. It should be boldly proclaimed that a Joshua phase is the *only way* to fulfill that potential. We must step over into our cultural destiny.

The law never succeeded in producing righteousness because sinful human nature was weak (Rom 8:3). Liberation alone will also never succeed in producing righteousness, because our sinful human nature is still weak. The liberation of our ungodliness has taught us that we could never live up to all our aspirations as a beautiful people apart from God's grace.

Part III

Roots and Fruits
of Consciousness

Chapter 10

A Little White Lie
in the Name of
Black Truth

T HE MILITANTS OF THE '60s were right to challenge the way we think. They were right to point out that if we are going to have a culture and a movement with any kind of integrity at all, then we must root it in Black history and experience. It is true that we could not afford to buy into an alien belief system, nor could we afford to accept the inferiority arising from it. Many still assume that Christianity is for Whites and Islam is for Blacks. But now that Islam is no longer an exotic novelty, Black thinkers generally consider themselves religiously neutral. If Christianity is the White man's religion, then surely it must be rejected in spite of our historic theological dynamic. But is Christianity the White man's religion?

To answer that question we will have to take a closer look at the nature of an *ethnic* religion. To be ethnic, a religion must have two characteristics. First, it must arise out of the historical experience of a people and take on itself their cultural identity. Second, its assumptions must be the basic commitment of the vast majority of that people. It must be woven into the fabric of the culture to such an extent that it seeps into the minds of the people without it needing conscious acceptance.

Although Western Christianity is somewhat expressed through Euro-American culture, Christianity itself did not arise in Europe or America. It grew in the Middle East among the people known as Hebrews. Its roots can be traced back to Adam.

In Genesis 3:15 God tells a fallen Adam and Eve that a liberator will come ("the seed of woman"). This liberator will conquer Satan (crushing the serpent's head), but the liberation will only come through the suffering of the liberator; his heel will be bruised. This is a primitive but accurate description of what Christ accomplished on the cross. Thus Christianity is disqualified as the White man's religion in the first sense, as its roots precede the White race by a long shot.

A European Dialectic

White society may appear to be Christian at a superficial glance, but on closer examination the picture radically changes. We must remember that as Western thinking grew and developed its roots were heavily influenced by Greek philosophy in the early stages and secular science in the later. Although Christianity played a major role in this development, and although many Europeans were indeed true to the Scriptures, the history of European thought in general has been one of rejecting the biblical world and life view and replacing it with the White man's religion. This rejection came about through a series of distortions of Christian theology on the part of Western philosophers.

Let's take a brief look at what happened. Again and again Christian thought would be opposed by some nonbiblical perspective, which modified it sufficiently to create in time a new religion. Hegel called this process of change a dialectic, and the two opposing forces the thesis and antithesis; the new "product" emerging from the struggle he called the synthesis. One of the first syntheses of Christian faith came when the Hebrew mind met the Hellenistic (Greek) way of thinking as it reflected on the Scriptures. The result was a scientific theology, an analytic and rational approach to Christian thought.

Augustine of Hippo (A.D. 354-430) was able to synthesize scientific theology with some of Plato's philosophical thinking. He expressed this in part in his pivotal work *The City of God*.[1] In it he compares the heavenly city, whose God is the Lord Jesus Christ, to the earthly city, whose citizens worship their own gods. Now Augustine contributed many good things to the development of Christian theology, and for these we can praise God; but he did have a weakness in his framework. And, unfortunately, the European rejection of the scriptural world view focused on it, transforming it into a major problem.

In Augustine's concept, the city of God was too closely identified with the church as an institution. This might at first appear to be harmless. However, it leaves room for a dichotomy between a *secular* realm, which is thought to be independent of God and his revelation, and a *sacred* realm, namely, the institutional church as "the peculiar instrument of God's gracious dealings with men." Such a dichotomy would not arise from a truly biblical world view. Scripture distinguishes between the church as the kingdom of God in a narrow or special sense, and creation as the kingdom of God in the broad, general sense. In the Bible, God reveals that his lordship is not limited to the scope of the institutional church. Indeed, he exercises his lordship over the whole creation in his plan of redemption.[2]

Because Augustine did not recognize that philosophical thought has its root in religious commitment, he was never able to develop a comprehensive Christian world view. He saw pagan philosophy and Christian theology as two unrelated fields. But this kind of dualistic structure is unscriptural.[3]

After Augustine, European theology evolved into medieval scholasticism, where theology was considered "the queen of the sciences," and the doctrine of the institutional church set the agenda for all learning. Scholasticism came out of a synthesis of Augustine's framework with the work of Thomas Aquinas. This synthesis "set into motion . . . the pattern of thought that was to dominate the Middle Ages, a pattern of 'nature' and 'grace' in which there was a dichotomy between the natural, earthly powers and the supernatural powers of the institutional church."[4] Augustine's ideas were gradually replaced by Thomas Aquinas's concepts, and the motif of "nature" and "grace" "made its entrance into [European] Christian thought."[5] Now the sphere of "nature" was considered to be independent from "grace," and the dualism in European thought grew even more acute.

With human reason elevated to a status equivalent with "grace," some thinkers began to consider "grace" irrelevant or unnecessary. Thus the "Age of Reason" began. Since that time European thought has looked to mankind as the final judge for all truth.

A completely mechanical view of "nature," with no room for personhood, resulted and began to threaten the European thinker. To keep things from getting worse, a desperate search was begun for a substitute for the lost concept of "grace." Rousseau, Kant and Hegel all came up with alternatives. By this time European thinking had completely cut itself off from God's Word. The result was rationalism, which considered human reason alone as the final authority for establishing truth. Remember the Flatlanders?

Next in this development of thought came the synthesis between rationalism and the Reformation. Their offspring was deism, a secular Christianity-ism. The deistic notion that God started the great machine of the universe and then stood back and did nothing about its inner workings provided fertile soil for the flourishing of European ethnocentrism, which saw the world revolving around Europe.

It is true that Europe did not have an exclusive hold on ethnocentrism. Every group, whether tribal, racial, cultural, political or geographical, has a strand of ethnocentricity. It comes from unrighteousness. What made European ethnocentricity so devastating was that it was able to assert its negative influence far beyond the boundaries of Europe.

We must remember that science, itself the result of a biblical view of our environment, had also been ripped from its biblical framework, secularized, and was thought to be independent from God. Such was the trend of almost everything in European thought by now. This secularized science yielded a blind technology gutted of all ethical restraints. It functioned as an ideal tool for European ethnocentric ambitions of expansion. This is what Nikki Giovanni identified in "The Great Pax White." For her this technology without ethics was what released destructive forces on the world, in the name of "peace"/"Christianity."

With the lordship of God having been thrown out of the arena of European thought, the way was paved for a synthesis between deism and European ethnocentrism. The result was White secular humanism, the view that White humanity is the source of truth and value. Behold the White man's religion: obviously it was not Christianity.

Ramifications of the White Man's Religion

The "un-gospel" of White secular humanism spread to the entire world as its domination was established and maintained by a prostituted technology. Every aspect of life was touched by this ethnic religion in its global expansion.

1. *Applied politically (outside Europe), White secularism became colonialism.* As colonies were established around the world, their political structures and geographical boundaries were determined by the politics of Europe. The colonialists had little or no concern for the natural ethnic groupings in those foreign lands. For example, sub-Saharan Africa was carved up by the colonial powers at the Congress of Berlin (1878) and the Conference of Berlin (1884-85). No Africans were present. The political bound-

aries that were fixed split some tribes and caused power struggles among others. Though most of these colonies are now independent nations, much of their political and tribal turmoil is due to those arbitrary boundaries which were dictated in the colonial era.

2. *Applied economically, secularism became mercantilism.* What colonialism did politically, mercantilism did economically. Though it did not work well for all European nations, mercantilism did serve the economic interests of the elite class in countries such as Spain, Portugal and France. Economic development for the benefit of the indigenous population never got very high on the agenda.

3. *Applied biologically, secularism became evolutionism.* Contrary to popular myth, evolution is not a proven scientific fact. It is a basic assumption forming a framework by which many biologists interpret and classify the differences in life forms. Creation is also a framework. Not all that passes for creationism is true to the creation framework; the same can be said for evolution. Unlike evolution, however, creation derives from God's Word. God was there at the beginning and man wat not.

An evolutionary account of biological variety assumes that differences within groupings are due to some being "higher" on the evolutionary scale than others. This is why an explanation of the origin of race consistent with evolution will lead to inequality and racism. On the other hand, an explanation of the origin of race consistent with creation will lead to human equality, because we are all in God's image. If an evolutionist is a racist, he is at least consistent with his framework. If a creationist is a racist, he is being inconsistent with his framework.

4. *Applied philosophically, secularism became materialism.* When Thomas Aquinas developed his "nature" and "grace" framework, he opened the door to materialism: Secularized "nature" became the preoccupation of the European thinker, and materialism emerged without a ripple. Once secularism was firmly established, self-gratification through accumulating wealth became a substitute for spiritual values. Often materialism turned into greed

as it tried to fill the spiritual emptiness left by the retreat of "grace."

5. *Applied sociologically (outside Europe), secularism became racism.* The roots of racism can be traced all the way back to Adam and Eve and their rebellion against God. When they set themselves up as final judge in all matters of good and evil, they were judging the Creator by the standards of the creature. In essence they were guilty of "creature-ism." Creature-ism today manifests itself as me-ism. Individuals set their selfish desires up as the standard for determining the worth of other people. A collective manifestation of the same creature-ism is racism, a simple extension of me-ism. One race sets itself up as the standard of judgment for all races.

6. *Applied culturally, secularism became imperialism.* If Western culture had kept the Word of God as the source of its values, imperialism would have been avoided. But the Bible had lost its central role in the West. Western culture itself became the standard by which to judge other cultures. Like racism and me-ism, cultural imperialism has led to a disrespect for other cultures and a failure to see truth—the grace of God at work in other cultures. Cultural imperialism was the root of the White bias that Black militants pointed out.

7. *Finally, applied as a cult (in America), secularism became White Christianity-ism.* This we have already discussed. When the advocates of Black militancy identified "Christianity" as the White man's religion, they were in fact identifying a cultic mutation of White secular humanism. This heresy originated as a justification of American slavery, which was itself a by-product of racism. The militants neither saw secularism as the basis of White Christianity-ism nor recognized unrighteousness as its root. Their analysis of racism, radical as it was, was not radical enough. It never dealt with the real root of racism.

Built-in Racism
By and large, the Bible-believing community had been blinded to the institutional evils in American society. This blindness is somewhat understandable. For example, how can one understand insti-

tutional sin, like racism, when the scope of sin has been limited to
personal issues, such as drinking, smoking or "chewing"? Furthermore, most members of the Bible-believing community belonged
to the middle class and middle-class life is highly individualistic.
How can you see evil in a system which delivered the goods so
efficiently? In his essay "The Web of Urban Racism," Harold M.
Baron wrote:

> Maintenance of the basic racial controls is now less dependent
> upon specific discriminatory decisions and acts. Such behavior
> has become so well institutionalized that the individual general-
> ly does not have to exercise a choice to operate in a racist man-
> ner. The rules and procedures of the large organizations have
> already prestructured the choice. The individual only has to
> conform to the operating norms of the organization, and the
> institution will do the discrimination for him.[6]

This unthought-out racism explains in part the social ineptness of
the Bible-believing community when it came to racial justice in the
twentieth century. It justified Malcolm X's condemnation:

> If the so-called "Christianity" now being practiced in America
> displays the best that world Christianity has left to offer—no one
> in his right mind should need any much greater proof that very
> close at hand is the end of Christianity.
>
> Are you aware that some Protestant theologians, in their writ-
> ings, are using the phrase "post-Christian era"—and they mean
> now?
>
> And what is the greatest single reason for this Christian
> church's failure? It is its failure to combat racism. It is the old
> "You sow, you reap" story. The Christian church sowed racism
> —blasphemously; now it reaps racism.[7]

It is White Christianity-ism which was bitterly denounced in the
militant movement of the '60s, and rightfully so.

But if Christianity is the White man's religion, why has it been
thrown out of the life of so many institutions in White society, such
as the public school system? What is the real, underlying religion
in today's society? It is not Christianity; it is secular humanism.

This notion of human independence from God has enjoyed an increasing position of authority in Western thinking since the Renaissance. The secular framework has left absolutely no room for the God of the Scriptures. Yet, unfortunately, Western society is still *called* Christian.

A Black Dilemma

The soul dynamic which emerged from our experience never developed such a notion of independence from God. The survival of this theological dynamic is a real testimony to the grace of God. It is worth noting that the theology of the Black church is oriented to the Old Testament. Part of the reason for this is the close similarity between the Hebrew and the Black experience. Both developed a covenant consciousness.

Biblical Christianity is by God's plan universal in nature; it can take on itself the identity of any culture. We see this universality of the gospel in the book of Acts. The day of Pentecost, when the gospel was preached in every language of the world, is clear proof that the Christian gospel is not locked into a particular culture or language. We see its universality as it was communicated and absorbed in Jewish and Greek cultures in the first century. The call of the church was to penetrate every nation, every culture, with the message of salvation, that all peoples might submit to God in their ethnicity. So, in Christianity, if I do not worship God *in my own culture,* I am being inconsistent with my faith.

Notice how unlike an ethnic religion Christianity is. In Islam, if I try to worship Allah in my own culture, I am being inconsistent with my faith! By Muslim teaching, the Qur'ān cannot be translated into another language without losing its "inspiration."

In the fact that Christianity intends us to worship God in our culture, we can see that the Black theological dynamic is a legitimate expression of the biblical message. It fully qualifies as Black, having historical and cultural continuity in the Black experience. This satisfies our need to be Black. Yet it does not have merely ethnic origins; it is rooted in the universal Word of God. This satisfies our need to transcend Blackness. One thing is clear: the theological dynamic does not qualify as the White man's religion.

It is a shame that the militant figures of the '60s failed to make this obvious distinction. Ironically, when they searched for a replacement for Christianity in their new movement, instead of escaping the White man's religion, they fell right into its trap. The militants tended to have more formal education than what had been historically attainable for Blacks, but that education was founded on Western thought, which by that time had infected even the Black colleges. Thus they chose the alternative supplied them: secular humanism.

In essence, then, the militants turned away from a valid Black expression of the universal Word of God. As a result they turned away from the only valid basis for the Black ethnicity they were trying to develop. They turned to secular humanism, a little "white" lie in the name of Black truth. And the Black movement degenerated from there into various do-your-own-thing-isms.

Too small. This new absolutized Blackness at first appeared to give fresh new meaning to our experience and culture, but the limitations of Blackness soon became visible.

Blackness became a particular type of abstraction and, like other such abstractions, it could not give a complete account of reality. Blackness as a symbol of oppression in White society and a symbol of pride in the Black community gave us valid understandings on history, sociology, psychology, economics and so on. But it could not give us, for example, an alternative understanding of math, physics or chemistry.

This presented a dilemma because the ideal of Blackness was supposed to be a universally valid absolute for our emerging cultural identity. Many went so far as to say that what could not be completely contained within Blackness was by definition White.

At first the Black ideal was liberating. But after it had been absolutized, it became a restricting Black box—a box which was unable to contain all the humanity to which the new Black movement had sensitized us. Later we discovered that even where the new Black consciousness had given us new insights, those insights were not comprehensive but perspectival; that is, they represented not objective truths, but the truth seen from where we stood.

When it was discovered that Blackness, as a limited ideal, was not big enough to be an absolute, the quest was on for a transcendent non-White absolute to buttress Blackness. Hence the turn to Islam. Others "bit the bullet" and gave up on Blackness as an ideal, settling merely for a Black style as they opted for materialism. Hence the emerging narcissism. The secularists and Muslims had accused Christians of being dualistic and self-centered, but now they too were opting for dualistic and self-centered structures.

Black *is* truly beautiful, but it is not beautiful as a god. *As a god it is too small.*

God's gift. Ethnicity has its beauty only as it derives from understanding that we are in God's image. Absolute ethnicity, like every other finite concept which is absolutized and cut off from God's revelation, will always end up crashing on the rocks of meaninglessness and chaos. Black identity will only have its real fulfillment when it is seen in light of how God is active in the world. Historic Black theology has always affirmed this truth. It is the power of this truth which has accounted for its remarkable survival.

The Word of God embraced in the Black theological dynamic has always given us a transcendent reference point for reflection on ourselves and on our situation. Whenever we seek to understand our situation without a transcendent reference point, we fail to find an answer to our crisis. The White man's religion has failed us. The Black version of the White man's religion has failed us. The Arab ethnic religion is failing us.

True ethnic identity will be impossible if it is based on ethnic identity itself. It is God who gave us the basis of the new Black consciousness. It is not a human invention. Yet, as we have seen, the militants abused it by secularizing and absolutizing it. Only the Scriptures will show us the true significance of Black consciousness. The theological dynamic is God's gift to our people, and it will lead us to develop a true ethnic identity.

Chapter 11

"Busting Out"

BASIC TO A RECONSTRUCTION of Black culture must be a more radical understanding of God's assessment of why we do what we do. We need God's assessment of man's basic religious commitment, which is the root of culture itself. Not religious commitment in the sectarian sense of belonging to a particular faith, but in the generic sense of the basic human attempts to solve problems in our relationship with the Creator. To find God's assessment of our condition, we must go to the Word of God.

Knowledge of the Nations
When our first parents began to experience the result of their hav-

ing rebelled against God, they did not run toward God first thing
and ask forgiveness, but ran and hid (Gen 3:7-8). This vain attempt
to get away from God was itself a religious act. In one way or another all people have been acting out this same religious tradition
ever since. Religion can be defined as the basic commitment to seek
or avoid God and his revelation in every area of life. Let's begin the
discussion of our basic religious commitment by seeing what
Scripture says about it:

Why do the nations rage
    and the peoples plot in vain?
The kings of the earth take their stand
    and the rulers gather together
against the LORD
    and against his Anointed One.
"Let us break their chains," they say,
    "and throw off their fetters."
The One enthroned in heaven laughs;
    the Lord scoffs at them. (Ps 2:1-4)

Here the nations of the world are seen involved in a futile conspiracy to rid themselves of God's authority, control and presence.
Although these nations are, by and large, without the Scriptures,
they know enough about God to plot rebellion against him and his
"Anointed One." How do they know all this?

It is often forgotten that, according to Scripture, people without
God's Word are not without God's revelation. Scripture is persist-
ent in its assumption that the nations without Scripture still have
extensive knowledge of God.

The wrath of God is being revealed from heaven against all the
godlessness and wickedness of men who suppress the truth by
their wickedness, since what may be known about God is plain
to them, because God has made it plain to them. For since
the creation of the world God's invisible qualities—his eternal
power and divine nature—have been clearly seen, being understood from what has been made, so that men are without excuse.
    For although they knew God, they neither glorified him as

God nor gave thanks to him, but their thinking became futile and
their foolish hearts were darkened. (Rom 1:18-21)
According to Paul, not only is God's character plain in our environment, but God himself is present in reality making it plain. Therefore all people perceive and understand God's "eternal power and
divine nature." So no human being can claim ignorance about God.
But the passage does not stop there; not only do all nations know
about God, but they know God himself.

Thus in Psalms 2:1-4, along with trying to extricate themselves
from God's authority and control, the nations are vainly trying to
avoid the presence of God. This is quite a serious indictment
against humanity and its basic religious commitment. Just how
extensive is human knowledge of God? To know that we will have
to take a closer look at the content of God's revelation which comes
to all people.

1. *God is.* Moses must have been somewhat startled when God
revealed his name as "I AM" (Ex 3:14). God was saying that his
existence is the most obvious and fundamental thing in human experience. There can be no IS without God's IS; and since IS is, God is,
because God is IS. God here introduces himself as the very bedrock
of all existence. Since all people experience existence itself, then
all people automatically experience God's existence.

The only way anyone can declare that God "ain't" is to declare
that IS ain't. And if IS ain't, there never was a "God ain't" declaration
in the first place. Without God, even the atheist could not say "God
ain't." He would not exist to say it. Without IS there would be
nothing. "The fool says in his heart, 'There is no God' " (Ps 14:1),
because the only way he could say "there is no God" is on the basis
of God himself. This dilemma is an aspect of what the theologians
call "the ontological problem." (*Ontology* is the study of existence
and being.) Duke Ellington, though not a theologian in the classical
sense, beautifully communicated this in his song "Something
about Believing" when he said, "the silliest thing ever read was
that somebody said 'God is dead'; the mere mention of the first
word automatically eliminates the second and the third."[1]

If, for example, a person accepts the existence of a building, he automatically accepts the existence of its foundation, because all buildings sit on something. This is so obvious that we don't have to think about it. There simply would be no building in the first place without some kind of foundation.

God has not left us just knowledge of his existence, however. He has gone beyond that to communicate the characteristics of his being and the nature of reality, and the Scriptures provide the key for discovering this natural revelation. They testify that they are the Word of God (2 Tim 3:16-17; 2 Pet 1:20-21), and in them we learn that God speaks both through Scripture and through the environment (Rom 1:20).

A person, let's say a humanist, may accept the fact that there is a foundation to all existence and yet deny that the God of the Scriptures is that foundation. He would be denying that the Scriptures are the Word of God. Or he may take another tack in his search for a haven from God's authority: He may accept some aspects of Scripture as true and reject others. For example, he may accept the scriptural teaching of a revelational environment and reject the Scripture's testimony that Scripture is revelation. He may even accept some of the scriptural self-testimony and reject the rest of it. No matter how he slices the cake, his decision as to which parts of Scripture are true and which false rests on the notion that he himself is the highest authority in determining truth. But if God is not the highest authority, then God is not God, by definition. The secular humanist has made himself the god, the reference point of existence.

I have argued already that if we deny God, we deny existence itself; and we end up with nothing. But we cannot talk about nothing because nothing is *nothing*. If we can talk about nothing, then nothing becomes *something*, but who or what is it? However, if we deny God, we deny existence itself, and we end up with nothing, and so on. The secular humanist has already eliminated the Scripture as the means of divine communication by his original denial that the Scriptures are God's Word. If he also eliminates the environment as revelation, he has eliminated the very possibility of revelation itself, because by definition a person never leaves his environment. Our environment is always where we are. And if there is no revelation of God in our context, there is no other place to see him. This brings us back to the nothingness of nothing.

Now since nothing is nothing, how can it be a higher authority than God? The humanist has therefore left himself with *nothing* as the basis of existence. But all that is based on nothing is nothing.

Therefore if our humanist appeals to "nothing" (or himself) as a higher authority than God, he is in deep trouble. As we saw from "the ontological problem," without God there would be no secular humanist in the first place. Oh, well! Back to nothingness.

All this reasoning is an aspect of what theologians call the epistemological problem. (*Epistemology* is the study of how we know what we know.) The epistemological problem flies in the face of the person who says that there is no absolute truth anywhere. If he denies the possibility of absolutes, his only alternative is to say that everything is relative. But this, of course, would mean that he had failed to escape from absolutes, for to say that all is relative makes relativism the absolute! It becomes the basis of do-your-own-thing-ism.

How does this understanding affect us in our quest for freedom and dignity? It reminds us that if we want a sound basis for a reconstructed Black culture, we had better start with what God says and work our way through our task, reflecting back on God's revelation in Scripture and in our own environment. Since Scripture teaches that God speaks through the creation, then Scripture should serve as the key to rediscovering what God says in our culture.

Having said that God is and that Scripture is our best source of revelation about God, we will use it now to see what we can know about God.

2. *God is the Creator.* Genesis 1:3-26 is pregnant with the phrase "And God said . . ." What does God say in the creative act? He says things like "light" (v. 3), "atmosphere" (v. 6), "water and land" (v. 9), "plants" (v. 11), "sun, moon and stars" (vv. 14-16), "sea

creatures and birds" (v. 20), "land animals" (v. 24), "man—male and female—in God's image" (vv. 26-27). These words are the obvious environmental realities that all human beings have in common. Since they are all expressions of God's creational word, they all say, "God is the Creator." "Long ago by God's word the heavens existed and the earth was formed" (2 Pet 3:5).

John 1:1-5 also follows this line of reasoning.

In the beginning was the Word, and the Word was with God, and the Word was God. He was with God in the beginning.

Through him all things were made; without him nothing was made that has been made. In him was life, and that life was the light of men. The light shines in the darkness, but the darkness has never put it out. (Jn 1:1-5 NIV and TEV combined)

Here the Word of God is pictured as being present with God from the beginning. It is God himself. John goes further to say that nothing came into creation that was not an expression of God's Word, and that all life and knowledge are derived from God's Word. The knowledge of God through his Word in creation (the light) has survived all attempts to snuff it out (the darkness).

Thus every aspect of our environment, including ourselves, relentlessly cries out, "God is Creator!" Even for the oppressed, whose environment has been corrupted by the oppressor, the message is "God is Creator, but he did not create things this way." Why? Because "the light still shines in the darkness" and this light undergirds the oppressed's resistance to oppression.

3. *God is the Sustainer.* "The Son is the radiance of God's glory and the exact representation of his being, *sustaining* all things by his powerful word" (Heb 1:3). "In [the Son] all things *hold together*" (Col 1:17).

The power of God's Word, his Son, sustains the whole creation. The fact that the creation holds together testifies that God is the Sustainer.

4. *God is glorious.* According to Scripture, every time anyone looks up, he or she sees the glory of God, his brilliance.

The heavens declare the glory of God;

the skies proclaim the work of his hands.
Day after day they pour forth speech;
night after night they display knowledge.
There is no speech or language
where their voice is not heard.
Their voice goes out into all the earth,
their words to the ends of the world. (Ps 19:1-4)

With an inaudible voice God reveals his glory in plain and understandable language.

5. *God is infinite and eternal.* "For since the creation of the world God's invisible qualities—his eternal power and divine nature—have been clearly seen, being understood from what has been made" (Rom 1:20).

It is clear to all, says Paul, that the nature of God puts him in a class all by himself. There is a sharp distinction between Creator and creature. God is divine and we are human; God is infinite and we are finite; God is unlimited and we are limited. God himself is "invisible" because he is too glorious, too bright, too vast, too perfect, too righteous to be seen with our limited and fallen sight.

6. *God is a righteous judge.* "The heavens proclaim his righteousness, for God himself is judge" (Ps 50:6). Anybody who sees the sky sees God's righteousness and his unique, divine qualification to be the ultimate judge of right and wrong.

7. *Human existence has eternal significance.* God's revelation to all peoples, even those without the Scriptures, extends beyond a knowledge of himself to an understanding of our human place before him. "He has . . . set eternity in the hearts of men; yet they cannot fathom what God has done from beginning to end" (Eccles 3:11).

All people know at the core of their being that they must deal with eternity. This is a function of being in the image of God. Though we have eternal existence in common with God, we remain different from God because he is infinite and we are finite. The real issue we wrestle with is not *if* we will exist forever but *how.* Will it be eternal life or eternal death?

8. We are unrighteous, and God's wrath hangs over our heads. "The wrath of God is being revealed from heaven against all the godlessness and wickedness of men" (Rom 1:18). Since God reveals his wrath from heaven, all people know they are guilty before him, the righteous judge.

9. We cannot save ourselves from God's wrath. The apostle Paul teaches that people without the Scriptures (the law) know what God requires.

> All who sin apart from the law will also perish apart from the law.... (Indeed, when [nations], who do not have the law, do by nature things required by the law, they are a law for themselves, even though they do not have the law, since they show that the requirements of the law are written on their hearts, their consciences also bearing witness, and their thoughts now accusing, now even defending them.) . . .
> "There is no one righteous, not even one;
>   there is no one who understands,
>   no one who seeks God.
> All have turned away,
>   they have together become worthless;
> there is no one who does good,
>   not even one." (Rom 2:12, 14-15; 3:10-12)

We know that we are guilty of not meeting our obligations. We know this by the light of God's Word shining in us. Is there anyone who is not guilty? No, "not even one!" Since there is no righteousness among fallen humanity, we have no hope of salvation—even in our best efforts—from the wrath and judgment of God. Without God's help we would be totally hopeless.

10. God has shown us favor we in no way deserved. He revealed his grace in creating the nations and giving them a chance to search for him, being close so they could find him, and sustaining them in spite of their sinful condition.

> From one man he made every nation of men, that they should inhabit the whole earth; and he determined the times set for them and the exact places where they should live. God did this

so that men would seek him and perhaps reach out for him and find him, though he is not far from each one of us. "For in him we live and move and have our being." (Acts 17:26-28) God reveals his grace in his patience toward all the nations. He has yet to execute the full wrathful judgment we deserve: "God . . . made heaven and earth and sea and everything in them. In the past, he let all nations go their own way. Yet he has not left himself without testimony" (Acts 14:15-17). God reveals his grace by meeting all our basic life needs. "He has shown kindness by giving you rain from heaven and crops in their seasons; he provides you with plenty of food and fills your hearts with joy" (Acts 14:17).

Since, according to the Scriptures, God's truth in creation is plain for all to see and God has ensured that all people will understand what his revelation says, then all people who have their five senses have a knowledge of God. They know that God is, that he is the Creator and Sustainer, that he is glorious, infinite and eternal, the righteous judge. They know of humanity that our existence has eternal significance, that we are unrighteous, having God's wrath hanging over our heads, and that we cannot save ourselves from that deserved wrath. But they also know that God has shown mankind favor that is not in any way deserved.

Prisons of Paganism
All people in the world have extensive knowledge of God. It is plain, however, that this knowledge is not universally acknowledged in all cultures. Why? The Bible implies the answer when it states that God's wrath is aimed at those "who suppress the truth by their wickedness" (Rom 1:18).

The Greek word *katechō*, translated "suppress," has both a positive and negative meaning. On the positive side it means to hold fast or lay hold of. But Paul uses the word here in its negative sense, meaning to "hold back," to "restrain." Here it means "holding in prison."[2]

Thus the Word of God is not universally acknowledged in the world's cultures not because the truth is not there, but because the truth of God is incarcerated in prisons of paganism. "Although they knew God, they neither glorified him as God nor gave thanks to him, but their thinking became futile and their foolish hearts were darkened" (Rom 1:21). They know God himself. God has shown them that he is a God of grace and that he is a God who deserves to be glorified (Acts 14:16-17). In spite of this, they do not give him that glory nor thank him for the grace. People refuse to take advantage of God's grace and therefore refuse to seek him (Rom 3:11-12).

Even though all knowledge is derived from God's Word, mankind tries to hold the truth of God's natural revelation hostage in anti-God frameworks. The result is anti-God "knowledge," which denies the revelation of God, the very source of knowledge itself. "Their thinking became futile and their foolish hearts were darkened. Although they claimed to be wise, they became fools and exchanged the glory of the immortal God for images made to look like mortal man" (Rom 1:21-23).

As I look around at our world, I see four basic anti-God frameworks, four prisons of paganism.

Suicidal religion: Man's attempts to solve his problem with God by *denying reality*. People do this by seeking either to eliminate their own existence or to radically alter it. The goal here is to come to an end so that we will no longer have to deal with God's wrath. The foundation of this religious prison is a refusal to acknowledge that human existence has eternal significance.

Suicidal religion is primarily found in the East, but it is also seen in our part of the world. Some Western examples are suicide, various Eastern-style mysticisms, drug and alcohol abuse (or just the attempt to get high), and militant shallowness (refusing to relate to others on a truly human level).

God-bribing religion: Man's attempts to solve his problem with God by trying to earn God's favor. Since God's wrath is revealed from heaven, this religious motif is, in essence, an attempt to bribe God into looking the other way when we come before him in judgment. The foundation of this religious prison is a refusal to acknowledge that God is a righteous judge and that we cannot save ourselves from his wrath. This religion is also based on a refusal to acknowledge the consequences of unrighteousness.

God-bribing religion is primarily found in the Middle East, but it is also seen in our part of the world in religions such as Islam, which promote reliance on works for righteousness, or in the widely held belief that "God helps those who help themselves."

Peek-a-boo religion: Man's attempts to solve his problems with God by trying to hide from God. The goal here is to shield ourselves from the wrath of God behind little gods, other human beings or some form of ritualism. Undergirding this religious prison is a refusal to acknowledge that God's wrath is inescapable.

Peek-a-boo religion is primarily found in Africa, South America and elsewhere in the southern hemisphere, but it is also seen in our part of the world. Some examples of it are animism, ancestor worship, idol worship, voodoo, astrology and "bureaucratic monotheism." Bureaucratic monotheism, an expression of African religious experience, has been described in Osadolor Imasogie's essay on traditional African religion:

> While Africans accord prominence to the divinities, the divinities are regarded as having been created and appointed ministers by the Supreme Being. However, the place given these divinities is so conspicuous that monotheism must be qualified in such a way that this prominence is maintained while the underlying monotheistic motif is not obscured. . . . This author, however, is convinced that the phrase "bureaucratic monotheism" best describes the African traditional religion. . . .
>
> It is common knowledge that in any bureaucratic system . . . the average citizen is more familiar with the officials who regulate his day-to-day activities than the king whom he seldom sees. Even though the ministers and officials derive their authority from the king, the ordinary citizen looks up to these officials rather than to the king for his needs. My contention is that this socio-cultural pattern of the African society becomes the paradigm by means of which the African expresses his religious experience.[3]

Originating in Africa, bureaucratic monotheism could be considered the Black man's religion. It is seen in our community among those who submit themselves totally to authoritarian religious figures.

Theicidal (God-killing) religion: Man's attempts to solve his problem with God by trying to eliminate God's existence or by de-deifying him in some way. The rationale here is this: if we can get rid of God, we will get rid of God's wrath. This religious prison is based on a refusal to acknowledge that God *is.*

Theicidal religion is primarily found in Europe and North America. We have met this character before in the White man's religion. Other examples of this religion are atheism, materialism and civil religion. This last occurs when people blur the distinction between God and country; for example, some in our country wrap God up in the American flag and present him as an American, supporting the American system.

A final religious view belonging to this category is love-is-god-ism. Here we find those who accept the love of God but totally ignore his wrath and those who equate contentless love with God. I shall discuss this theicidal religion in chapter thirteen.

The Gospel Held Hostage?
All four of these anti-God religions show up as forms of Christianity-ism. Let's look at each again in this light.

Suicidal Christianity-ism describes people who strictly forbid the mind from entering into their Christian walk. The goal of this distortion is to eliminate all thinking out of fear of being "intellectual." It results in a kind of liver-quiver religiosity. People in this camp confuse man-centered thinking with thinking itself. Biblically speaking, there is nothing wrong with being intellectual. The mind is no more sinful than any other aspect of a human being, and to negate the mind is to negate a part of our humanity. The same could be said about denying emotions.

God-bribing Christianity-ism points to those who think they obligate God to show them favor for the good things they have done.

They think that because they go to church so many times, pray so many prayers and so on, God will do something for them in return. It results in a doctrine of works righteousness. By this they do violence to the grace of God. God's grace is not a response to our goodness; we have none (Is 64:6). We can only respond to God's grace (Tit 3:5). It's not that we first loved God, but that God first loved us (1 Jn 4:19).

Peek-a-boo Christianity-ism labels those who submit to the dictates of a religious tyrant. They see him or her as a substitute Christ. They let the tyrant do all their thinking and explain away his shortcomings. The result is a spectator-sport religion. The Jonestown tragedy exemplifies this heresy at its worst. Peek-a-boo-ism is characteristic of Black Christianity-ism, too. It is one thing to respect people in authority; it is another to hide from God behind them.

Theicidal Christianity-ism includes those who try to squeeze God into a mold or reduce him to some kind of system. For them, God can be manipulated. Those who identify God with only one race of people are also guilty of this distortion. White Christianity-ism is one of several such theicidal groups, including the Dutch Reformed Church in South Africa. In such instances the people worship Baal, not God, for Baal is the local or ethnic lord.

Application or Pollution?
When the gospel is applied to a particular culture, the result is Christianity. There can be as many varieties of Christianity as there are cultures, but these cultural Christianities would not contradict one another. They would have a complementary relationship as they focused on God's gracious deliverance accomplished in Christ. Hence it is not necessarily wrong to have a White Christianity or a Black Christianity.

Christianity-ism, on the other hand, is a Christianity that has been polluted by the paganisms of its culture. It attempts to hold the gospel hostage. Every culture where Christianity functions has a tendency to drift toward Christianity-ism.

The White man's religion is not a unique pagan prison. All cul-

tures of the world, including Black culture, have their own variation of paganism. Secular humanism did not fail us just because it
was the White man's religion. It failed because it is a vain attempt
to deny that God is. Islam is not failing us merely because it is the
Arab ethnic religion. It is failing us because it refuses to acknowledge our inability to save ourselves apart from the grace of God.
Islam is failing because all our righteousness is a total failure. And
peek-a-boo religion is not failing us merely because it is the "Black
man's religion." It is failing us because it refuses to acknowledge
the inescapability of God's wrath.

How can we prevent this pagan pollution? The various Christianities must balance between spiritual unity and cultural diversity,
just as different cultures interact, borrow from each other and
blend. We cannot allow cultural variation to become walls of cultural isolation as they have in South Africa. In an atmosphere of
cross-cultural fellowship, the pollutions of Christianity-ism in my
culture will often be more clearly seen by someone of another culture; we all have blind spots.

Our soul dynamic, for example, has aspects that have survived
from Africa. Some of these are positive, but not all of them. We
must build our culture by selecting those Africanisms compliant
to the Word of God. On the other hand, we must not be afraid to
contextualize the gospel. Jesus himself should be our example. He
was a Jew, but he did not come in the name of Judaism. He came in
the name of the Father. If we are Christian, we should be active in
our cultures, not in the name of Christianity-ism or Christianity,
but in the name of Christ.

God's Success

The only basic religious commitment that will not fail us is one of
seeking God rather than avoiding him, and that is only possible on
the basis of God's grace. We live as God's guests on God's turf. God
is Lord, and he simply will not let man's sinful plots frustrate his
ultimate purposes in the world. In fact, God does and will frustrate
every negative conspiracy that mankind tries to implement. God's

revelation is always "busting out" of man's prisons of paganism. This is why God laughs and scoffs at these plots, because it's like a gnat trying to take on an elephant in a wrestling match. For God has decreed that even "the wrath of men shall praise [him]" (Ps 76:10 RSV).

> The God who made the world and everything in it is the Lord of heaven and earth. . . . He himself gives all men life and breath and everything else. From one man he made every nation of men, that they should inhabit the whole earth; and he determined the times set for them and the exact places where they should live. God did this so that men would seek him and perhaps reach out for him and find him, though he is not far from each one of us. "For in him we live and move and have our being." (Acts 17:24-28)

Against the backdrop of a totally negative religious commitment, a commitment to avoid God, this is an astonishing statement by the apostle Paul. He seems to go against the stream of what he so clearly set forth in Romans 1 and 3. In the Acts record he says that the nations were created by God so that they would seek him and find him, in spite of their universal practice of paganism. Paul says further that God is not far from any of us because we live our whole lives in him.

If all the nations try to hold God's truth hostage, then how could they be seeking God? Paul's statement that God still gives us "life and breath and everything else" (Acts 17:25) should give us a clue. He alluded to this in Acts 14:16-17: The answer is God's grace, which he showers on all people. It is by God's grace that we seek God. He sends rain on the justified and the unjustified (Mt 5:45).

Good News

If we are going to succeed in rebuilding our culture, then it must be based entirely on the consciousness that God, by his grace, is active in the world today. Solely because of God's active grace many people are able to commit themselves to seek God and his revelation. These are the people who by God's power will confess to him their lost and hopeless condition and throw themselves on God's grace as their only hope of deliverance from wrath.

As we have noted, the driving force which gives rise to every culture is religious in nature. But for fallen man, apart from God's grace, that religious commitment is always negative, an effort to avoid God. However, because God graciously frustrates evil, those who practice negative religion will never succeed in avoiding God's Word in any area of life (Ps 139:7-8, 11-12). Because of God's grace, we can have a positive religious commitment; however, because God's gracious work is not yet complete, we do not yet consistently seek God in every area of life (Phil 3:12). Those who seek God by his grace are the ones in whom the history and destiny of a nation will ultimately be fulfilled (Rev 7:9-10). Jesus called them the salt of the earth and the light of the world (Mt 5:13-14). They are the hope of the nations.

We can now see what causes culture to well up in the life of the nations. It is this dynamic interplay between these positive and negative religious undercurrents over which God exercises his gracious lordship. Knowing this, we will understand why a culture's noble aspirations are due to the grace of God. With this knowledge we will understand that people betray and fall short of their noble aspirations because of their unrighteousness (Rom 3:23).

The unique message of the Scripture is that God has indeed provided for the solution to our problem with God. This message is stated throughout the Scriptures. From an Old Testament perspective the message was that God *will* accomplish deliverance for his people. From a New Testament perspective, the message is that God *in Christ has* accomplished deliverance for his people and that they can begin to experience this deliverance now. This is good news to all who by God's grace seek him.

Chapter 12

"That Boy
Sho' Can Preach!"

T HUS FAR I HAVE only touched on soul dynamic. In this chapter
I want to explore its characteristics further by comparing it with
what we think of as formal theology. I would like also to look at
new roles that the dynamic can play as we reconstruct Black culture.

Because music is key to the theological dynamic, music will be
the basis of this discussion.

Tone and Rhythm
Much of God's Word came to us through singing—the Psalms; the
Song of Songs; the lyrics of Deborah, Moses, Hannah and Mary;

the Hosannahs sung by the crowd when Jesus triumphantly entered Jerusalem. Like the Israelites of the exodus who sang when they saw the hand of God at work in their midst, our people during slavery also sang about God's work among them. We have noted that many Black spirituals, with their double messages about the kingdom of God and freedom from slavery, related the slaves' understanding of how God would deliver them from bondage.

Not only the words, however, reflect our theology; the music also mirrors our understanding of God's divinity and the world's future. Music is a function of theology, and to do theology is to apply God's Word to all areas of life. Theology—formal, systematic theology and our own casual-as-an-old-pair-of-sneakers beliefs—finds expression in our music. And the songs that we moan and groan shape our ideas of God and his world.

The two main components of music are tone and rhythm. These have always been part of our revelational environment. God created us to musically express beauty and truth to his glory. Song could serve as a parable of reality. We cannot, however, compose or perform music employing *all* the possible combinations of tone and rhythm in *all* possible modes of unity and diversity, form and freedom, any more than we can know all the mind of God. We are finite. Only the infinite, triune God of the Scriptures can create perfect music.

In God's music, form and freedom are conterminous, each being the ultimate fulfillment of the other, but in our music they are not. Either form serves freedom, or freedom serves form. We have retained our musical ability since the Fall, but, like the image of God in us, our music is marred by sin. Because of sin we should have had not music but simply noise, where unity and diversity are subject to chance. It is only by God's grace that we have true music rather than mere noise. In our music we catch glimpses of God's creative image in us and of our original potential.

As we saw in chapters ten and eleven, when people submit themselves to God's lordship, they have dignity. But when they attempt to set themselves up as the absolute, their humanity breaks down. Likewise, as long as music remains an expression of the glory of God, of truth and beauty, the music retains its dignity. But when music is absolutized, becoming its own end, it breaks down into noise.

Two Approaches
There are essentially two approaches to music, the formal and the dynamic. We call them *classical* and *jazz*. We know what classical music is: It is the little dots, circles and lines of Beethoven and Brahms that come to life when a conductor stabs the air with his baton. These sounds that fill the air are not the conductor's or the violinists'. They belong to Beethoven and Brahms. The beauty of a classical piece is found in the mind of the composer, in the music as it is written. Thus the goal of the classical musician is to repro-duce—as faithfully as possible—the sounds the great composers had imagined. Only in rare moments and clearly marked cadenzas do classical musicians improvise. Their main task is not to impro-vise but to imitate.

Jazz is different. The beauty of jazz is found in the soul of the musician and in the music as it is performed. Jazz is improvisa-tional. Just as classical music has developed musical composition into a fine art, so jazz has cultivated musical improvisation into a fine art. The notes that fill the air do not belong to a deceased com-poser; they issue from the vibrant souls of great performers like "Diz," "Byrd" and "Lady Day."

As it is with music, so it is with theology. Theology bears analogy with music in that it too can be approached as formal or dynamic. The two modes reflect two aspects of God's nature. Like classical music, the classical approach to theology comprises the formal methods of arranging what we know about God and his world into a reasoned, cogent and consistent system. Classical theology inter-acts in critical dialog with the philosophies of the world. It investi-gates the attributes of God and communicates primarily through a written tradition.

If the classical approach to theology has been called "the queen of the sciences," then the jazz approach to theology could be called "the queen of the arts." It investigates God's dealings with people in the joys and trials of daily life. This improvisational approach is illustrated in the soul dynamic. The jazz approach is not so much concerned with the status of theological propositions as with the hurts of oppressed people. It is not so much communicated by literary tradition as by oral tradition. And it is not so much concerned with facts as it is with life skills, knowing *how* rather than knowing *that*.

Jazz theology is a participation in the basic patterns revealed in biblical life situations. It inquires not only *what* God did and said, but *how* he said and did it. Furthermore, it expects him to do it again in a similar way in our lives: "Didn't my Lord deliver Daniel? Well, I know he can deliver me." Effective Black preachers respond to current situations by *theologizing creatively on their feet*, just as jazz musicians improvise new music and enliven old songs in response to the feelings and needs of the moment.

Classical theology and classical music reflect God's oneness. The unity of God's purpose and providence is reflected in the consistent explanations and consonant harmonies of classical music and classical theology. The genius of classical theology is in theology *as it was formulated*.

But God is not just classical. God is jazz. Not only does he have an eternal and unchanging purpose, but he is intimately involved with the difficulties of sparrows and slaves. Within the dynamic of his eternal will, he improvises. God's providential jazz liberates slaves and weeps over cities. Jazz can be robustly exultant or blue; God has been triumphant and also sad. Jazz portrays the diversity, freedom and eternal freshness of God. The genius of jazz theology is in theology *as it is done*.

Even the divine name, I AM, carries aspects of both classical and jazz theology. To the classical theologian, God's name means "I HAVE BEEN WHAT I HAVE BEEN." To the jazz theologian he is "I WILL BE WHAT I WILL BE."

"Let's Have Chu'ch"

Jesus was a master jazz theologian. The Bible says that "the crowds were amazed at his teaching" (Mt 7:28). The emphasis here, as can be seen from the context, is not on the substance or content of his teaching (*didaskalia*), but the act or skill of the teaching method (*didachē*). Jesus brilliantly transformed historic scriptural teaching into living contemporary parables. He used the art form of the Scriptures themselves. He evoked in the hearts of his hearers an intuitive knowledge of God—a knowledge which God placed in them by grace. In his delivery of the Father's precious truths, he artfully appealed to the people's common sense and experience. "His words had the ring of authority" (Mt 7:29 Phillips). It ain't just what he said but the way how he said it.

The best Black preaching is analogous to Jesus' use of short phrases and parallelisms as we see in the Sermon on the Mount (Mt 5—7). This jazz approach sweeps listeners into verbal and emotional responses. I can imagine that many folks said of Jesus, "That boy sho' can preach!"

Jesus' conceal-to-reveal technique with parables enticed listeners to listen with their hearts and to participate in the teaching. In other words, they "had chu'ch." So powerful was Jesus' skill that even the cops sent by the Pharisees to "bust" him returned empty-handed, explaining, "No one ever spoke the way this man does" (Jn 7:46).

I am not saying that the content of Jesus' teaching had nothing to do with his power as a teacher. Indeed, his teaching was unique in that his content and skill were both equal and ultimate. For a rabbi in the first century the development of one memorable parable was the pinnacle of achievement which demanded many years of academic sweat. But along came Jesus with his jazz approach, speaking over sixty such parables!

Jesus' jazz teaching maintained a constant variety of fresh, picturesque imagery; he didn't let the culture or people numb the teaching. Culture tends to respond to truth the way we respond to a joke. A joke is hilarious when first heard, but told repeatedly it just gets boring. Likewise a parable's initial effectiveness decreases with successive hearings: a culture numbs itself to truth. Jesus flooded culture with his parables. People could not escape the implications. Truly out of his belly flowed living water (Jn 4:14).

Jesus' use of parables shows one way his teaching style was like jazz music. It was experiential and improvisational in nature. But it was jazzlike in other ways, too.

What You Know Is What You Do

The dynamic concept of knowledge, as the word is used in Scripture, also parallels the jazz-classical distinction. Jesus criticized the scribes, saying, "You err because you don't know the Scripture!" Certainly they knew the Scriptures in great detail. But they knew them in a detached manner. Jesus spoke of knowledge in terms of intercourse. You can see then, said Jesus, how "every scribe who has been trained for the kingdom of heaven is like a householder who brings out of his treasure what is new and what is old" (Mt 13:52 RSV).

At the height of the Festival of Shelters, Jesus went to the temple and began teaching (Jn 7:14-15). The Jews were amazed and remarked, "How does this boy know all this? He has never been to seminary." Jesus was not a "doctor of the law," yet by his teaching he showed himself to be a doctor in his own right—a person with knowledge unattainable in the seminaries.

For years the Black church has conferred on its outstanding preachers the title of doctor. This is a recognition, consistent with a biblical concept, that knowledge is not just something that can be attained at school. It can be found in life. While the facts of classical theology are formally taught, the skills of jazz theology are dynamically "caught."

The great advantage of the jazz approach to theology is its requirement that people be involved with Truth. "If anyone wants to *do* God's will, he will *know* . . . my teaching is from God" (Jn 7:17 Phillips). Jesus delivered to his disciples all that the Father had given him. But he did not give his disciples a course outline and a

lecture. Instead he began portraying truth in his own life. He did
not give his inquirers a bibliography; he said, "Follow, imitate and
be involved with me" (see Mt 9:9; Mk 1:18; 8:34; Lk 5:11; Jn 1:40,
43). Choosing twelve men to play out the drama of discipleship, he
told them that the ultimate goal of being taught was to be like the
teacher (Lk 6:40). This concept of knowledge-as-lived is demonstrated in Jesus' life. It shows a second way jazz theology illumi-
nates Christian experience.

More Than Music
The jazz approach can also illuminate how we understand the inspiration of Scripture. It is sometimes difficult to understand how,
for instance, the four Gospels can all be inspired when each of them
is unique, incorporating certain traits of its author. But when the
Holy Spirit breathes the gospel through Matthew, Mark, Luke and
John, it is like Dexter Gordon playing the same tune on his sax on
four different occasions. Every time he plays it, he makes changes
in his riffs. Does that mean that any one playing is not musically
superb and consistent with the other performances? Does it mean
that he had not played the same piece four times—that he has, in
fact, played four different pieces?

In a similar way there is complete "harmony" between the
musicians in a jazz combo. The performance of "On Green Dolphin
Street" by the Miles Davis Sextet serves as an excellent illustration
of the jazz harmony among the Gospels.[1] In this renowned performance, harmony was based on (1) the underlying chord progressions, (2) a specific rhythm and (3) the musicians' quest for excellence. Among the four Gospels, harmony is based on (1) the person
of Christ as the content and meaning of the gospel. (2) the Holy
Spirit as the agent of inspiration and (3) our quest for God's fullness
as he transforms us, and our culture through us.

The improvisations of Miles Davis on trumpet, Cannonball Ad-
derley on alto sax, John Coletrane on tenor sax and Bill Evans did
not break the rules of musical harmony. On the contrary, these
musicians, "carried along" by rhythm, fulfilled the rules in an

open, lucid and dynamic way. They were "inspired" *within* the chord progressions. Similarly, the unique arrangement of events in Matthew, Mark, Luke and John did not break the rules of historic harmony. On the contrary, these evangelists, *inspired* by the Holy Spirit, fulfilled the rules in an open, lucid and dynamic way. They were *carried along* within the parameters of infallibility and inerrancy.

In "On Green Dolphin Street" Bill Evans on piano introduces and develops the theme. Miles, Trane (John Coletrane) and Cannonball also improvise from their stylistic perspectives. Among the four Gospels, John introduces and develops the theme from "the beginning." Matthew, Mark and Luke reveal Christ from their cultural and theological perspectives. When the four evangelists share the same narratives, there are relatively few differences in the texts. But like these jazz musicians who have distinctive differences in their solos, the evangelists have distinctive differences in their arrangement of the facts when they did not share the same narratives.

The instruments of Miles, Trane and Cannonball are monotonic, and in a sense they could be considered *synoptic* because of their similarity. Each of their instruments, however, has a distinctive range: soprano (trumpet), alto sax and tenor sax. When these men improvise they add dimension to the beauty of the performance because of their differences.

The books of Matthew, Mark and Luke are called synoptic Gospels because their texts are similar. However, Matthew addresses himself to Jewish readers, Mark to Romans and Luke to Greeks; the distinctive perspectives of the audience show up in the presentations of the life of Christ. Since these three evangelists also write from their own perspectives, they add further dimension to the revelation of Jesus because of their differences.

The rhythm line also illustrates the relationship between inspiration and revelation. Paul Chambers on bass provides rhythm at various levels of tone, while Jimmie Cobb on drums provides rhythm where tone remains relatively constant. The Holy Spirit reveals Christ at various levels of revelation while he provides us with inspiration that remains constant.

Bill Evans on piano demonstrates unique capabilities as he plays chords. With one stroke he is able to cover as much ground as Miles, Cannonball and Trane do in the flow of their riffs. Similarly, John's Gospel has multiple levels of theological depth. It is simple yet profoundly sophisticated. Though John gives several levels in understanding Jesus, his Gospel weaves the body of Christ together in spiritual union. John gives "chords" of depth to our understanding of Jesus.

The New Testament writers have, like jazz musicians, demonstrated something positive, namely, "soul"! Jazz is more than music. It's a way of doing. Through jazz theology Black preachers participate in a basic pattern set by God in the act of revelation. Jazz theology helps us apply God's Word to every area of life and culture.

Chapter 13

Cultural Seeding

J AZZ THEOLOGY AND classical theology are not mutually exclusive. Just as George Gershwin and the Modern Jazz Quartet wed the freedoms of jazz to the forms of classical music, so biblical scholars may marry the intuitive spirit of jazz theology to the rational principles of classical theology.

Solid, classical orthodoxy provides limits within which we may improvise, even as musical keys and chord progressions guide the jazz musicians. It tells us what God is like and what he is not like. It keeps us from error and excess. However, it does not keep us awake because it does not have the power to blast us out of the "paralysis of analysis."

You may sleep through a symphony, but most people will pay attention to a jazz riff. Jesus calls us to stay awake and be involved in the movements of the times. That is what jazz theology does. It involves us where the "nitty" meets the "gritty." It tells us that God is on the move, that the kingdom is coming. And since the kingdom is coming, it tells us how to get ready. We need to get ready. Our culture is in trouble. Jazz theology can equip us to revive it.

Dr. King's application of the theological dynamic to desegregation provided the jazz-theology basis for the southern Black church to play the key role in the civil-rights movement. The northern church had nothing comparable in its fight against institutional racism. It developed no theological base for involvement in the Black movement. The northern church's involvement tended to be social, not theological. Jazz theology could have made the difference for the northern church.

In turning to Islam, northern thinkers choked off the very possibility of a jazz theology for its faithful. Islam is strictly classical; it does not allow for improvisation. In Islam all non-Arabic culture and language are excluded. Even within Arabic culture Islam frowns on nontraditional phrasiology, leaving the Muslim with doctrinaire repetition and cold orthodoxy. There is no room for soul.

Song of the Soul

As Black music once expressed our spiritual life in the days of slavery, so it still does, but it paints a bleak picture. The music of our day has been shaped by the soul dynamic, but it does not have the hope of the Black spirituals. In popular Black music, we no longer sing of the promised land, the deep river or the sweet chariot. Our music once reflected a life lived from Sunday to Sunday as it looked expectantly toward the everlasting Sunday of freedom and dignity. But with the secularization of Black culture, the music has come to portray a life stretched thin between one brief romance and the next. The spirituals have become the blues.

Today's Rhythm and Blues (R and B) is the most influential

fountainhead of the cultural dynamic. Millions of young people live by the music. They carry radio/tape decks with them all day long. They skate to the solitary music of their headphones and cruise to the blaring accompaniment of their car stereos. What they hear shapes their lives and ours. What does the popular music say to them?

Though the Black church no longer sets the musical trends, we still find theological phrases woven into the lyrics of recent Black music. A couple major trends in R and B developed in the '70s. The first trend considered God as the source and lord of love. I call this God-is-love-ism. In his 1971 album *What's Goin' On?* Marvin Gaye expressed a seemingly genuine turn toward God.[1] The album was rich in Christian themes. Selections such as "Wholy Holy" and "God Is Love" had lines like "Jesus left a long time ago. He left us a book to believe in and in it we've got a lot to learn," and "Don't go talking about my father, God is my friend." The album became a hit.

Other artists, such as Stevie Wonder, Eddy Kendricks and Earth, Wind and Fire, began recording albums with similar themes. Stevie Wonder became by far the most influential artist of this trend with his albums *Music of My Mind, Talking Book, Inner Visions, Ful-fillingness First Finale,* and *Songs in the Key of Life.*[2]

A second trend in R and B might be called love-is-God-ism. Songs of this trend use spiritual terms as code words for secular love. In a perverse, inverted manner *born again* and *moving with the spirit* (along with the soul dynamic these terms reflect) are taken to have sensual overtones. They have come to mean "having a new lover" or "engaging in sex outside marriage." These phrases have become familiar in our culture, but it is their secular meanings that are influencing and undercutting our culture, not their spiritual meanings. In his later album, *Let's Get It On* (1973), Marvin Gaye picked up on these secular meanings.[3] His title selection concludes with the line "[Let's] get sanctified." Here a theological term refers to sexual arousal.

The jazz theologian must affirm and fulfill the positive aspira-

tions of God-is-love-ism while counteracting love-is-God-ism. The
apostle Paul did this on Mars Hill. He affirmed the truths of Epimenides while exposing the pagan nature of Greek philosophy and
religion (Acts 17:22-34).

Response to our culture demands more than simply a reprise of
"The Old Rugged Cross." What we need is an injection of the biblical world view into our culture. I call this *cultural seeding.*
Simple, basic, fundamental truth must be planted in our culture
before the fruit of the gospel can ripen. This is what Jesus did with
his jazz parables. This is also what Martin Luther King did with his
ethics dramatizations. Rhythm and Blues today is a key cultural
fountainhead into which seeds of God's truth must be planted.

However, a simple return to the old music—even the old spiri
tuals—would be merely in the classical mode. We need to return
not to the spirituals but to the *spirit* of the spirituals. In that spirit
theologians and musicians can craft an artistic and creative response to the needs and crises of our age. Through cultural seeding
in R and B we can begin to revive the soul dynamic and reconstruct
Black culture.

Even though we referred to the Blues as negative, we may also
see the Blues in a positive light. The Blues remains one of the most
influential phenomena in the development of our culture. Though
other American musical forms have gone through radical changes,
the Blues themes in our music have been consistent. Many which
describe the relationship between a man and a woman are parallel
to the covenantal themes found in the prophets, such as Jeremiah,
Ezekiel and Hosea. Here God plays the role of a husband speaking
to his unfaithful wife (God's people). Because we are a "Blues people," we have great potential of response to God who in the Old
Testament preceded us in singing the Blues.

Involved Obedience
We need to re-examine Jesus as a jazz theologian and use the Scriptures as he did. He lived portraying his teaching. If we can do this,
we will fulfill the aspirations of the historic theological dynamic

and lay the foundation for a new generation of Black leadership to emerge.

Through jazz theology we can become equipped to enter culture at all levels and to portray God's truth in the living, dynamic style of Jesus.

We now go to Hillside Baptist synagogue where the sermon of Dr. J. C. Davidson is already in progress.

Jesus: And what's the use...

People: Yeah!

Jesus: in calling me, "Lord, Lord"...

People: Well!

Jesus: if you don't do what I say?

One man: Look out, preacher!

People: (laughter)

Jesus: Let me show you what a man is like...

People: Uh, huh!

Jesus: who only hears what I say...

People: Com' on now!

Jesus: and doesn't do it.

One man: Better leave that one alone, doc!

People: (laughter)

Jesus: He's like a man who built his house...

People: Talk to me!

Jesus: and laid his foundation...

People: Uh, huh!

Jesus: on soft earth.

One man: I know you gone to meddlin' now, doc.

People: (laughter)

Jesus: When the storm came...

People: Say that!

Jesus: down came the rain,...

People: Yeah!

Jesus: up came the flood...

People: Yes suh!

Jesus: and the house fell in...

People: My lawd!
Jesus: in a great noise.
People: Mercy!
Jesus: But the man who does what I say...
One man: Go 'head.
Jesus: is like a man, building a house,...
People: Wha' chu' say!
Jesus: who dug down to rock bottom...
People: Help yo'self.
Jesus: and laid the foundation on it.
People: Yes suh!!
Jesus: And when the storm came...
People: Well! Well!
Jesus: down came the rain,...
People: Take yo' time.
Jesus: up came the flood.
People: Preach it!!
Jesus: But the house was like a tree...
One man: Talk to me, doc.
Jesus: planted by the water.
People: My lawd!
Jesus: It could not be moved.
People: Oooooh! Thank you, Jesus!
One man: It's all right to preach.
People: Good God a'mighty!!!

A'nt Jane and Miss Sally walk away from the meeting after the service.
Miss Sally: Honey, that boy sho' 'nough came through today!
A'nt Jane: Yeah, honey chil', them scribes and folks ain't *never* preached like *that!* Mmmm glory! We sho' had chu'ch today.
(Luke 6:46-49, contextualized)

Part IV

Toward a
New Agenda

Chapter 14

New Vistas

$\mathbf{M}$ANY OF US HAVE achieved a greater degree of liberation than our people have ever had, but are we truly liberated? We saw in chapter three that the closer a people get to liberation, the more their own ungodliness and God's judgment will show.

This point is often overlooked by advocates of liberation. Liberation alone is not enough. Liberation is insufficient if it is not accompanied by a quest for godliness in every area of life. Liberation alone will lead to self-oppression because a liberated ungodliness will always do its thing, and that thing is sure to bring death (Rom 6:23).

This, however, should not excuse us to give up the fight for liber-

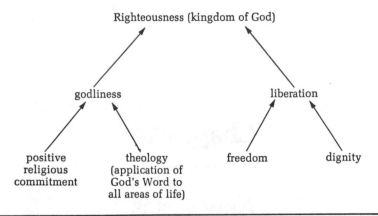

Figure 11: The Kingdom of God.

ation. We should fight for liberation *because* it is not enough. We should seek it in order to see our need for godliness. Human liberation and godliness are two sides of the same coin; the coin is the kingdom of God and his righteousness (figure 11). This is why Jesus said we should seek the kingdom "first" and "all these things [freedom and dignity] will be added." Liberation as a lens to see God's righteousness is the freedom and dignity we have pursued in historic quest. Godliness as a perspective on God's righteousness involves doing theology with a commitment to seek God.

Not a Right but a Power
Righteousness includes liberation. Righteousness will never liberate ungodliness to do its thing. Righteousness, both collective and individual, will lift a people above the frustrating effects of ungodliness and give them the will and power to realize their loftiest aspirations (Mt 5:6). The quest for righteousness in every area of life must be on the top of the Black agenda if we are to become the people God created us to be (Mt 6:33).

The more an oppressed people seek to construct their resistance to oppression around the Word of God, (1) the stronger will be the cultural power generated by their struggle, (2) the greater will be the likelihood that the oppression will be broken, (3) the smaller will be the likelihood that the resistance movement will be destroyed by the ungodliness of those involved in it, and (4) the smaller will be the likelihood that they will lose their cultural cohesion and compassion for their fellow human beings. This was the dynamic that gave Dr. Martin Luther King's leadership of the civil-rights movement such cultural power.

The less an oppressed people seek to construct their resistance to oppression around the Word of God, (1) the weaker will be the cultural power generated by their struggle, (2) the smaller will be the likelihood that the oppression will be broken, (3) the greater will be the likelihood that the resistance movement will be destroyed by the ungodliness of those involved in it, and (4) the greater will be the likelihood that they will lose their cultural cohesion and compassion for their fellow human beings.

I believe that the secular Black movement splintered into many fragments because it sought to do away with God and his revelation. This explains also why, when some of our people began to "make it," they became wrapped up in the new me-ism. Because their own ungodliness was never challenged when it resurfaced, they lost their compassion for those who remained in the under class.

True liberation "is not the right to do what I want, it is the *power* to do what is *right.*"[1] If we are going to achieve the liberation of our historical quest, then we must go *beyond liberation* to righteousness—God's righteousness. Not the "holier than thou" brand of self-righteousness, nor religiosity, but an applied righteousness lived out in all aspects of culture.

Where Do We Go from Here?
In Part II we discussed several phases of our historic quest for liberation: Colored, Neo-Colored, Negro, Neo-Negro, Black and Post-Black. We discussed the fulfillment of these phases, identifying it as the Joshua phase. There has never been a more critical time in

our history than *now* for the implementation of this phase. But what shape should the Joshua phase take? If Malcolm and Martin were like Moses in pointing us toward the promised land, then what Joshua will take us in?

First of all, our entry into the promised land must involve both our collective and individual identities. The biblical world and life view, expressed through an expanded and revitalized soul dynamic, can make this possible. The Old Testament covenants could not produce righteousness because the Righteous One had not yet been revealed. Yet the concept of the covenant was valid. It foreshadowed the coming of the Messiah. Where Adam, Seth, Noah, Abraham, Moses and David failed, Jesus succeeded.

The historic phases in our quest could not produce true freedom and human dignity. Yet the soul dynamic which came from it is valid. Black history is not over yet. Where the Colored, Neo-Colored, Negro, Neo-Negro and Black phases fell short, the Joshua phase can succeed.

Southern-stream desegregation was not the ultimate answer for Black America. But the application of the soul dynamic is key in providing the *basis* of life in the promised land. Northern-stream nationalism was not the ultimate answer for Black America. But cultural nationalism is key in providing the *shape* of life in the promised land.

"Christ is the end of the law" (Rom 10:4). Jesus said that the whole Old Testament pointed to him (Jn 5:39-40). So the Joshua phase will be the fulfillment of our historic quest. Our whole inheritance points to it. The Joshua phase must apply the soul dynamic to the issues now confronting us. We may enter into dignity with surefootedness if we enter with Jesus, if we let his Spirit lead us in righteousness.

A Renewed Dynamic

Northern-stream thinkers were concerned not just with justice but with power, not just with desegregation but with nationalism. The theological dynamic could have been applied in the northern situation, but the militants feared that a theological approach would mean accommodating to racism. So instead of taking advantage of this powerful, God-given resource, northern thinkers were left fighting over the crumbs which fell from the barren tables of secular humanism (the White man's religion) and Islam (the Arab religion). The northern stream can only be reconstructed through the principle God showed us by Brother Martin's example.

To apply the theological dynamic to our contemporary situation, two things must happen: (1) we must revitalize the fading dynamic with a fresh injection of biblical illumination, and (2) we must expand the dynamic by addressing it to all our cultural concerns and issues. This is the challenge and opportunity especially for Black Christians. But what characteristics must they have to bring forth this renewed theological dynamic?

In Israel there was a tradition of Spirit-filled, "ecstatic" prophets, men like Samuel, Elijah, Jehu, Gad, Nathan and Obadiah. Their usual method of prophecy was singing with musical instruments backing them up (2 Kings 3:15-19). These prophets lived on the love offerings of the people. The tradition was eventually corrupted and prophet "unions" were formed to legislate standardized prophets' fees. These later official prophets were merely trying to milk the ecstatic prophetic tradition for all they could get.

God raised up a new prophetic movement, referred to as the "poetic" prophets, which included Isaiah, Jeremiah, Ezekiel, Daniel and Amos. Often these new prophets were not a part of the official prophetic clergy (Amos 7:13-14). Their prophecies employed puns, and they often pronounced God's judgment on the unionized prophets (Jer 23:9-40).

Black history has included an antebellum tradition of Spirit-filled preachers. Their usual method of preaching has been "toning" and "whooping" with an organ or piano, while a toning congregation backs them up as they interact with each other. These preachers were often the only ones able to keep our people going from week to week. They lived on the love offerings of the church. Today, in some cases, the tradition has been corrupted. Some preachers are merely milking the tradition for themselves (me-ism). Fortunately there is a righteous remnant of uncorrupted whooping preachers.

God may be raising up a new movement of jazz theologians to stand beside the traditional preachers who have not been cor-rupted. Together they will be equipped to disciple the Black cul-ture in new and creative ways.

Restoration and Expansion
Unlike the northern Israelite kingdom whose people were oblit-erated, the southern kingdom saw a remnant restored to the land of Canaan. To that restored kingdom Jesus came and began his har-vest of the righteous remnant of Israel.

Unlike the northern stream whose power has disintegrated, the southern stream is still with us because the Black church is still with us. In a context inspired by a renewed Black church, Spirit-filled jazz theologians can begin a harvest of new cultural prophets more powerful than Malcolm and Martin. These prophets will point our people toward new vistas of righteousness.

In earlier times the church pulled in the majority of our people. Today it involves a plurality. While the church is still our single most powerful institution, there are now significant groups of people who would be involved in our historic quest but who are beyond the range of the traditional church. These include people who are primarily concerned with broad cultural issues (such as poverty and justice) and those who focus on personal self-disci-plines (such as diet and self-control). The first group has been left stranded by secularism while the second group has been marooned by Islam.

It would be inappropriate to attempt to bring both these groups into the culture of the traditional church. Nor need we try to trans-plant existing Black Christianity into either subculture. We need instead to develop a fresh approach to applying the good news to these contexts. We need a new mode of Black Christianity—a mode which, among other things, would include models of the Black church correspond to these subcultures. Such new manifestations of the church, incidentally, would not necessarily be all Black. Certainly we should not want to replace the traditional church. But with the addition of new models of the church, the cultural range of the church at large will be greatly expanded to once again involve a majority of our people. Thus we would be in a better position to expand the theological dynamic.

Jazz theologians will be the ones who revitalize the theological dynamic. Those who have had theological training on the classical side need to transfer that knowledge to the jazz side. In doing that, we gain a new appreciation for the wisdom of A'nt Jane. We also re-establish the relationship between the nuggets of the theological dynamic and their corresponding passages of Scripture. With its revitalization the dynamic could be more effectively passed on to succeeding generations. Its survival would be ensured.

Chapter 15

The Fields Are
Black unto Harvest

T HE JAZZ THEOLOGIAN must actualize what we have learned from both streams of our history as well as what we will learn through an ongoing process of revitalization, expansion and application of the soul dynamic. The renewed dynamic will provide the reason for doing it. The renewed dynamic will provide the ethical basis for doing it. And the renewed dynamic will provide the means for identifying and resisting unrighteousness.

As the jazz theologian begins to apply the revitalized and expanded theological dynamic to all aspects of our culture, a practical righteousness will begin to emerge—an intracultural righteousness to overcome our ungodliness, and an extracultural righteousness to overcome oppression.

How can we facilitate the emergence of this Joshua phase? Where do we begin? Whatever the shape of the Joshua phase, it must be undergirded by an ongoing process of education and realization.

Education: To Know Who We Are and Who We Should Be

Rootlessness is one of the great problems of today's generation. In spite of the great renaissance begun in the '60s, the youth of Black America lack a working knowledge of our history.

The optimism of the '60s is partially at fault here. It assumed that the succeeding generations would carry on the struggle with our same sense of urgency. Those who made this assumption forgot that each generation's response to its situation is based on its own perception of what is and what should be. With many of the superficial manifestations of racism gone, the new generations have no appreciation for what it took to remove them. Do-your-own-thing-ism and me-ism thwart any attempt to motivate our people to move forward. While education will not fully instill in them our old sense of urgency, it will help to prevent each generation from seeing itself in historical isolation.

Another factor contributing to today's sense of rootlessness stems from the lack of an adequate framework in which to view and understand the facts of our cultural history. Secular humanism proved inadequate because of its finite reference point, and Islam is proving inadequate because it excludes all non-Arabic culture and does not acknowledge our need for God's grace. Only the soul dynamic can provide an authentic framework for self-understanding. It is indigenous to the Black experience, yet it is derived from God's Word, which speaks to every cultural and historical situation.

We saw in chapter twelve that, while education involves knowledge, knowledge involves not just facts but skills. Education must not only teach the facts of our history, consciousness and destiny from a scriptural perspective. It must also teach the skills to analyze and actualize this knowledge in terms of God's Word.

Cultural unrighteousness assaults us from all sides. It especially overwhelms the young and impressionable. Countless times children are raised in the church only to be lost to the pagan practices of today's secular culture. This is unacceptable. We must equip our children both with a biblical world and life view and with the skills to outthink their counterparts with "sound reasons for the hope that is within them." We must also equip them with the wisdom to influence their culture through such avenues as Rhythm and Blues and the media. Otherwise we have little hope of saving our youth from the erosion of secularism.

To prevent this erosion and to help develop a new generation of Black leadership, we need to commit ourselves to the task and invest in alternative models of schooling. The public school system as it stands reeks with humanism. Not only that, but it functions primarily not to educate or inform, but to *conform* our youth to a secular value system which only serves the interests of the elite who call the educational shots. Neither the long-term nor the short-term interests of our community are served by these schools. As long as we depend on the public school system (in its present condition) as our primary means of education, we will not get far in establishing or implementing an agenda for righteousness. Without alternative schooling and a substantial commitment to change things in the public schools, we will continue to see the erosion of the positive values which made us strong.

In some cases we will have to replace the public schools with full, private schools, both large ones and home models. In other cases we will have to develop supplemental educational programs for those who remain in the public school system. These would provide workshops to teach such skills as reading, math, critical thinking and computer literacy, and to engage students in such studies as Black history, jazz theology, economics, Bible, community development and contemporary cultural issues.

While churches may want to form coalitions to develop private schools, most individual churches already have the facilities necessary for supplemental schools. If they have Sunday schools, then why not also have Saturday or after-school workshops? Why not borrow a page from the book of the Jewish synagogue, and involve young people on Saturdays as they do in "Sabbath schools"?

Whatever the case, we must avoid duplicating the fiasco of what often passes for Christian education today. In too many cases it consists of secular education with a bit of private salvation squeezed in the gaps. In too many cases Christian education has merely been a smoke screen used to maintain segregation in the classroom.

To develop effective alternative schools, we must completely rethink the learning process itself and develop innovative curricula which truly reflect a wholistic, scriptural world and life view. Also, because there is more to education than schooling, we must develop, recognize and affirm alternative ways of doing education—modes like community projects, guided study and apprenticeships.

Both traditional and new-model churches could develop these modes of learning and encourage mentors. Churches with vision, by joining forces, could sponsor symposiums, consultations and conferences to bring together educators who share the vision of a Joshua phase. Once an educational agenda has been worked out, we could seek the cooperation of other educational institutions, such as Christian colleges willing to be committed to actualizing our educational agenda. They could implement programs to help develop new mentors and enrich our pastors.

We must remember that Jesus taught us that what you *know* is what you *do*. Whatever modes of education we choose, our goal must be, among other things, to instill in the next generation commitment to righteousness, to goal orientation and to excellence.

Commitment to righteousness. As we have already seen, a dedication to righteousness is key to the fulfillment of the historic quest for liberation. Not only so, but the intensity of a people's commitment to righteousness is directly related to the effectiveness and wisdom of their leadership.

Commitment to goal orientation. Since losing the momentum of the '60s, no cultural goals any longer capture the imaginations of our people. We wander in circles because we are not setting and pursuing righteous goals. Given the lingering effects of the slave experience, this is understandable. The veto power of slavemasters rendered goal setting absurd at best. Somehow we have never fully overcome the "present orientation" that slavery precipitated. Though we are no longer in physical chains, in some ways we are still in cultural chains. If we do not form the habit of setting and pursuing righteous goals, we will condemn ourselves to a treadmill of merely reacting to unexpected oppressions.

When the desegregation of the South became our goal, it caught the imagination of millions, both Black and White, across the country. It became a powerful demonstration of the kingdom of God and his righteousness before the watching world. We need the vision of new, righteous goals.

Commitment to excellence. Programs like PUSH-excell try to instill in our young people a sense of excellence, and they are to be commended. However, excellence for its own sake will prove an inadequate stimulus for the required discipline. Only in the diligent pursuit of righteous goals can a quest for excellence and self-discipline be fulfilled. Because the goals of the civil-rights movement were the heartfelt convictions of so many, they generated the discipline to remain nonviolent in the face of vicious police dogs and bone-crushing fire hoses.

Realization: Renewed Institutions

Having begun to lay the foundation of righteousness through truly Christian education, we can complete the foundation by rebuilding our cultural institutions. We need to revitalize cultural life from the basic family unit through the political sphere.

Family life. The breakdown of the family is probably the greatest tragedy of our contemporary experience. From the creation, the family unit has been the main institution by which culture is instilled in succeeding generations. Reconstruction of Black culture will be impossible without restoring a strong Black family. The family must be the root of goal orientation and commitment to righteousness and excellence. I have been impressed with the strong sense of family I see, for example, in the Asian-American community. We need to learn from our Asian friends and emulate their example of family life where appropriate.

The intracultural aspect of the Joshua phase must involve a rediscovery and application of the scriptural teaching on manhood, womanhood, the marriage relationship, fatherhood and motherhood. We also need to overcome the disastrous effects of me-ism and do-your-own-thing-ism with regard to sex. We must teach the beauty and fulfillment of sex within the context of God-centered marriage. Every goal we set as well as everything we do in pursuit of these goals must place a premium on strengthening family units.

Body life. Truly the Black church body has played a key role in our history. Though we need to develop additional models of the church, we must also broaden the ministry of the traditional church. While Black preaching has been a priceless resource, traditional preaching alone is not adequate to prepare our people to meet the challenges of our day.

Our churches must function as extended families. They must bring families together and help them prepare each new generation for the responsibilities of marriage and parenthood. There are far too many fatherless children among us. The renewed church as an extended family could play a crucial role in providing models of manhood for our children.

The church must once again play a prominent role in education and realization. The new models of the Black church must take the lead, helping the traditional church to do the same. Then the church would be not only the bearer of good news; it would be that good news for individuals and families.

Economic development. The oppression we face today is less racially based than economically based. We have seen for the first time the complete cleavage between Blacks in the middle class and those in the under class. During the '60s the "White flight" from changing city neighborhoods was a symbol of racism. Today we are seeing a Black flight. The new classism is rooted in economics.

Me-ism among many of the new Black members of the middle

class has led to the pursuit of opulence and a corresponding lack of concern or compassion for those locked into the under class. As the church expands its prophetic role in our community, it must address this economic problem. But where do we begin?

We are a nation of consumers, and so consumer economics should be our starting point. We must develop strategies to stretch our consumer dollar and increase our consumer power. We can do it through such basic things as using sale items and generics, to forming buyer co-ops, to selective boycotts aimed at changing the policies of businesses whose practices hinder our pursuit of righteousness. We also need to develop and patronize businesses committed to building a Black economic base in and around our cities.

But it is not enough for us to remain a community of consumers. We must also become producers. To do this we must borrow a page from Booker T. Washington and "cast down the bucket where we are." We need to match our cultural resources to our economic opportunities. With proper education and a keen sense of economics, we can build employee-owned industries. These industries should range from food and clothing to construction and retail distribution. We should also develop new and creative service industries and, for cultural seeding, communications, information or media industries. Whatever the economic directions we choose, our goals must be to improve the quality of life in the Black nation and to soften the blow of institutional classism.

This task will indeed require wisdom and insight. It can be done if we can develop economists who will help us develop an economic base. Without a solid economic and righteous base, the resources which come to us will dissipate, without benefiting those who really need it. This is what happened to the Great Society programs of the '60s. If the proper economic institutions were in place, we would not be so vulnerable as we are today to the whims of the federal government.

Political cohesion. While the exercise of cultural power has far greater effect on society than political power, a little political savvy is crucial if we want to eliminate the institutional oppressions of today. We can truly be thankful for the work of the Congressional Black Caucus. But, as we noted in chapter seven, we need to do work like this at state and local levels of government also.

We must never let our cultural goals become allied with political liberalism or conservatism. The real issue for us is whether those who hold political office have a commitment to social justice and a righteous compassion for the oppressed. At those points we can form coalitions with them regardless of their broader stance.

We can't wait to see if sympathetic political leadership will emerge by coincidence. We must do all we can to develop and elect this kind of leadership. This means, among other things, massive Black voter registration, voter education and voter facilitation. We must also follow Brother Martin's example in finding new, creative ways to apply the theological dynamic to raising politicians' consciousness to issues concerning the righteous liberation of the oppressed.

Lift Every Voice
The infrastructure growing out of doing theology in these areas of cultural education and realization would put us in a position to meet the cultural challenges we face. It would lay the foundation for the Joshua phase. But what would a fully functioning Joshua phase be like? Certainly not a static state of existence, but a dynamic state of becoming. It would be a process of pursuing God's righteousness—a pursuit made possible only by grace and a deep love for God. This is why the Joshua phase must be theological. The state of becoming is the fulfillment of what Brother Malcolm illustrated by his life.

The Joshua phase should not be limited to Black people only. It should transcend Black culture as it has a redemptive effect on America at large. The cross-cultural aspects of the Joshua phase would help keep it from being spoiled by Christianity-ism.

The Joshua phase may have worldwide implications. It has amazed me to see how people all over the world seem to have positive feelings toward our people. For example, when the Iranian hostage crisis was at its height, the Ayatollah Khomeini ordered the release of Black hostages. I believe the favor we have with Third World nations is God-given. It is also worth noting that most cultures of the Third World are jazz-sided like ours. This gives us a distinct advantage in communicating the good news to the world. Black culture embodies a dynamic system of language. And the Black experience has enabled our people to more easily establish rapport with Third World and oppressed people. Recognizing these facts, Wycliffe Bible Translators, for example, has begun asking especially for Black recruits.

Given the current climate of the shift from Western missionaries to Third World church leaders, Black jazz theologians might be the only ones who can still go into the whole world without creating hostilities. A Black man was the last one to carry the cross of Christ (Mt 27:32). Black Christians might be the last ones to carry the cross of worldwide cultural discipleship.

Not all Black people will be part of the Joshua phase. Only two Israelites who left Egypt made it to the Promised Land. The Joshua phase is an opportunity for our people who are willing to pursue the kingdom of God and his righteousness.

These are the last days of the lull before the second wave of the Black quest. We are in the eye of a hurricane. Will the foundation of the second wave be a framework of righteousness to maximize its effectiveness? Or will we just do nothing, and watch Black frustration increase? Will we follow Christ as Lord and realize our cultural destiny, or will we reject Christ and face judgment?

We now stand at the fork in our historic path. We can fulfill our historic aspirations, following the path of righteousness leading toward the Joshua phase, or we can betray these aspirations, following the path of unrighteousness which deteriorates to terrorism. Which way will it be, Black America?

Let us move toward the Joshua phase! If we do, we will be empowered to participate in a great harvest as we proclaim the full counsel of God with a clarity and power never seen before (Acts 20:27). "For God has allowed us to know the secret of his plan, and it is this: he purposed long ago in his sovereign will that all human history [including Black history] should be consummated in Christ, that everything that exists in Heaven or earth shall find its perfection and fulfilment in him" (Eph 1:9-10 Phillips).

O the depth of the riches and wisdom and knowledge of God! How unsearchable are his judgments and how inscrutable his ways!

"For who has known the mind of the Lord,
    or who has been his counselor?"

"Or who has given a gift to him that he might be repaid?"
For from him and through him and to him are all things. To him be glory for ever. Amen. (Rom 11:33-36 RSV)
Maybe it was a vision of the Joshua phase of our history that inspired James Weldon Johnson to pen the words of our Black national anthem:

Lift ev'ry voice and sing
Till earth and heaven ring,
Ring with the harmonies of Liberty.
Let our rejoicing rise
High as the list'ning skies,
Let it resound loud as the rolling seas.
Sing a song full of the faith that the dark past has taught us,
Sing a song full of the hope that the present has brought us.
Facing the rising sun of our new day begun,
Let us march on till victory is won.

Stony the road we trod
Bitter the chast'ning rod
Felt in the days when hope, unborn, had died.
Yet with a steady beat
Have not our weary feet
Come to the place for which our fathers sighed?
We have come over a way that with tears has been watered,
We have come treading our path through the blood of the

    slaughtered.
Out from the gloomy past,
Till now we stand at last
Where the white gleam of our bright star is cast.

God of our weary years,
God of our silent tears,
Thou who hath brought us thus far on the way;
Thou who hast by Thy might
Led us into the light,
Keep us forever in the path, we pray:
Lest our feet stray from the places, our God, where we met Thee,
Lest our hearts, drunk with the wine of the world, forget Thee.
Shadowed beneath Thy hand,
May we forever stand
True to our God,
True to our native land.[1]

The fields are Black unto harvest.

Notes

Chapter 1: Toward a Promised Land
[1]Martin Luther King, Jr., *Why We Can't Wait* (New York: Mentor, 1963), back cover, his emphasis.

Chapter 2: Picking Up the Pieces
[1]Frederick Douglass, *Narrative of the Life of Frederick Douglass: An American Slave* (New York: New American Library, 1968), p. 120, my emphasis.
[2]By humanism I do not mean humanitarianism, which is the affirmation of the dignity of human beings. We should all be humanitarian. But humanism, as we shall see, leads to the erosion of the very possibility of humanitarianism.
[3]Denis Osborne, *The Andromedans and Other Parables of Science and Faith* (Downers Grove, Ill.: InterVarsity Press, 1977), pp. 29-31. Used by permission.

[4]*Lausanne Occasional Papers No. 2, The Willowbank Report—Gospel and Culture* (Wheaton, Ill.: Lausanne Committee for World Evangelization, 1978), p. 6.

Chapter 3: "Oh, Freedom!"
[1]James Cone, *Black Theology and Black Power* (New York: Seabury Press, 1969).
[2]Because of gravity, the air around us weighs about fifteen pounds per square inch. This is called air pressure, and it pushes on everything equally on all sides. When a wing passes through the air, the air flowing over the top travels faster than the air flowing under it. This causes the pressure on top to be less than the pressure on the bottom. The wing is pushed up as a result, causing lift.

When the upward pressure is greater than the downward pressure and the weight of the plane, the plane flies. This upward pressure is due to gravity, and so the lift of the wing is an expression of the law of gravity.

Chapter 4: Soul Dynamic
[1]Ray Dillard, professor of Old Testament, Westminster Theological Seminary, Philadelphia.
[2]Edward W. Blyden, *Christianity, Islam and the Negro Race* (Edinburgh: Edinburgh Univ. Press, 1967), pp. 114-15.
[3]Scholars B. F. Wright and M. A. Smith have confirmed that Augustine was born of African parents. Actually, Augustine, Tertullian and Origen were brown North Africans and not black sub-Saharan Africans. They have been classified as Caucasian by some. However, if these men had been Americans, they would have been classified as Black, and it is the American classification that I use here.
[4]Blyden, *Christianity, Islam and the Negro Race,* p. 114.
[5]Charles H. Wesley, *In Freedom's Footsteps,* International Library of Negro Life and History (New York: Publishers Co., 1968), p. 7.
[6]Chancellor Williams, *The Destruction of Black Civilization* (Chicago: Third World Press, 1976), pp. 101-2, 156-58, 164-65, 208-18.
[7]Columbus Salley and Ronald Behm, *What Color Is Your God?* (Downers Grove, Ill.: InterVarsity Press, 1981), pp. 18-19.
[8]LeRoi Jones, *Blues People* (New York: William Morrow, 1963).
[9]Salley and Behm, *What Color Is Your God?* p. 20, their emphasis.
[10]Ibid., pp. 20-21.
[11]An illustration often used by Dr. Henry Mitchell, author of *Black Preaching* (New York: Harper & Row, 1970), and *Black Belief* (New York: Harper & Row, 1975).

[12]Charles Tabor, "Is There More Than One Way of Doing Theology?" *Gospel in Context* 1, no. 1 (January 1978):6.
[13]James Cone, *God of the Oppressed* (New York: Seabury Press, 1975), pp. 54-55, my emphasis.

Chapter 5: A Formative Phase
[1]Lerone Bennett, Jr., *Before the Mayflower* (New York: Penguin Books, 1962), pp. 183-84.
[2]A fuller discussion of Jim-Crowism is found ibid., pp. 220-41.
[3]Thom Hopler, *A World of Difference* (Downers Grove, Ill.: InterVarsity Press, 1981), pp. 157-74.
[4]Walter Rauschenbusch, *Christianity and the Social Crisis* (New York: Macmillan, 1907).
[5]The idea of Prohibition, a ban on alcoholic beverages in America, can be traced back to the colonial years. However, it was encapsulated in the charter of the "Prohibition Party," organized in 1869 in Chicago. The party was never politically successful, but its philosophy infiltrated other social institutions. The ascendency of Prohibition was largely due to the influence of fundamentalism. It generally increased in popularity through World War 1 and culminated in the passage of the Eighteenth Amendment. This Amendment banned the manufacture, importation, exportation, transportation and sale of alcoholic beverages. Among the fundamentalist groups which became identified with Prohibition was the Women's Christian Temperance Union.

As it turned out, national Prohibition was unenforceable. It never succeeded in eliminating the alcoholic beverage industry. It only succeeded in driving the industry underground, facilitating the proliferation of organized crime. Prohibition was repealed in 1933 by the Twenty-first Amendment. This represented a major repudiation of the cultural influence of fundamentalism, since fundamentalism had so closely identified with it.
[6]The Scopes Trial is sometimes referred to as the Monkey Trial. In 1925 John T. Scopes, a high-school biology teacher in Dayton, Tennessee, was accused of teaching Darwin's theory of evolution in violation of a newly passed state law prohibiting "high school and college teachers from teaching theory which denies . . . creation." The prosecution included such notables as William Jennings Bryan, who was a leading fundamentalist lawyer and political leader. The defense included Clarence Darrow. The trial attracted worldwide attention.

The fundamentalist side won. John Scopes was found guilty and fined $100. But the trial revealed the inadequate intellectual savvy of its fundamentalist adherents. Though the fundamentalists won the battle, they lost the war, as their cultural and intellectual respectability plunged in the years which followed.

[7]Andrew E. Murray, *Presbyterians and the Negro: A History* (Philadelphia: Presbyterian and Reformed, 1966), p. 3.

[8]Lenard Broom and Norral Glenn, *Transformation of the Negro American* (New York: Harper & Row, 1965), pp. 9-15.

[9]Salley and Behm, *What Color Is Your God?* p. 32.

Chapter 6: Two Streams

[1]"The Atlanta Exposition Address, 1895," in *Black Protest Thought in the Twentieth Century*, ed. Francis L. Broderick and August Meier (Indianapolis: Bobbs-Merrill, American Heritage Series, 1971), pp. 4-6.

[2]Malcolm X with Alex Haley, *The Autobiography of Malcolm X* (New York: Grove Press, 1964), pp. 40-41.

[3]Ibid., pp. 53-54, his emphasis.

[4]Salley and Behm, *What Color Is Your God?* pp. 46-47.

[5]Ibid., p. 47.

Chapter 7: "De Lawd"

[1]Martin Luther King, Jr., *Stride toward Freedom* (New York: Harper & Row, 1958), p. 33.

[2]Ibid., pp. 43-44.

[3]Ibid., p. 46.

[4]Ibid., p. 54.

[5]Ibid., p. 56.

[6]Ibid., p. 59.

[7]Ibid., pp. 59-60.

[8]Martin Luther King, Jr., *Strength to Love* (Cleveland: Collins World, 1963), p. 151.

[9]King, *Stride toward Freedom*, pp. 61-63.

[10]Ibid., p. 63.

[11]Ibid., pp. 69-70, 84.

[12]King, *Why We Can't Wait*, p. 25.

[13]Ibid., p. 50.

[14]Ibid., pp. 76-95.

[15]Ibid., p. 61.

[16]Material in italics from King, *Why We Can't Wait*, p. 101; other material is from "Bill Moyers' Journal," PBS, interview with Andrew Young, aired on WHYY Philadelphia, 2 April 1979.

[17]King, *Why We Can't Wait*, p. 30.

[18]Ibid., p. 39.

[19]John Frame, Lecture Outline: "Doctrine of the Christian Life" (Philadelphia: Westminster Theological Seminary, 1979), p. 112, his emphasis.

[20]Ibid., pp. 112-13.

[21]King, *Why We Can't Wait*, p. 112.

[22]"Bill Moyers' Journal," 2 April 1979.

[23]King, *Strength to Love*, pp. 147-51.

[24]Ibid., p. 151.

[25]Columbus Salley, address to the National Black Evangelical Association (NBEA) Convention, New York, 1970.

[26]King, *Strength to Love*, p. 27.

[27]King, *Why We Can't Wait*, pp. 123-24.

[28]J. M. Kik, *Church and State in the New Testament* (Philadelphia: Presbyterian and Reformed, 1962), p. 46.

[29]King, *Why We Can't Wait*, p. 34.

[30]John Frame, Lecture Outline: "Doctrine of the Knowledge of God," Part 2 (Philadelphia: Westminster Theological Seminary, 1976), p. 3.

[31]Ibid., p. 4.

[32]Frame, "Doctrine of the Christian Life," p. 1, my emphasis.

[33]Cornelius VanTil, *Christian Theistic Ethics*, In Defense of the Faith, vol. 3 (Nutley, N.J.: Presbyterian and Reformed, 1977), p. 87.

[34]Stokely Carmichael and Charles V. Hamilton, *Black Power: The Politics of Liberation in America* (New York: Vantage Books, 1967), p. 55.

[35]Louis E. Lomax, *To Kill a Black Man* (Los Angeles: Holloway House, 1968), p. 190.

[36]George Breitman, ed., *Malcolm X Speaks* (New York: Ballantine Books, 1965), p. 74.

[37]Quoted from "Bill Moyers' Journal," 2 April 1979.

Chapter 8: "A Shining Prince"

[1]Eldridge Cleaver, *Soul on Ice* (New York: Delta, 1968), p. 74.

[2]Lomax, *To Kill a Black Man*, p. 121.

[3]Salley and Behm, *What Color Is Your God?* p. 65.

[4]*Autobiography of Malcolm X*, pp. 4, 2.

[5]Ibid., pp. 36-37, his emphasis.

[6]Ibid., p. 37.

[7]Ibid., pp. 154-55.

[8]Ibid., p. 155.

[9]Ibid., pp. 156-59, his emphasis.

[10]Ibid., pp. 163-64.

[11]Ibid., pp. 165-67.

[12]Ibid., p. 295.

[13]Ibid., p. 303.

[14]Ibid., p. 381.

[15]Ibid., pp. 339-41, his emphasis.

[16]Ibid., p. 365.

[17]Breitman, *Malcolm X Speaks*, pp. 63-64.

[18]*Autobiography of Malcolm X*, pp. 368-69, his emphasis.

[19]VanTil, *In Defense of the Faith*.

[20]Quoted in *Autobiography of Malcolm X*, p. 454.

[21]Cleaver, *Soul on Ice*, p. 59.

[22]Betty Shabazz, ed., *Malcolm X on Afro-American History* (New York: Pathfinder Press, 1970), p. 2.

[23]*Autobiography of Malcolm X*, pp. 432-33.

[24]Ibid., p. 434.

[25]Breitman, *Malcolm X Speaks*, pp. 76, 24.

[26]Lomax, *To Kill a Black Man*, p. 172.

[27]Breitman, *Malcolm X Speaks*, pp. 43-44.

[28]Carmichael and Hamilton, *Black Power*, pp. 37-38, 44.

[29]"Niggers Are Scared of Revolution," *The Last Poets*–Douglas 3, East Wind Associates.

[30]"STOP" (a song), lyrics and music by Henry Greenidge, 1970, sung by Soul Liberation.

[31]Breitman, *Malcolm X Speaks*, pp. 76-77.

[32]See Thom Hopler, "The Dynamics in the Black Church: The Interaction of Pan-Africanism, Church Growth, and Foreign Missions in the American Black Church from 1790-1975," "The First 25 Unbelievable Years—1875-1900," and "Review of the Black Missionary Effort," three unpublished papers, Fuller Theological Seminary, 1974-75.

[33]*Truth Is on Its Way*, Nikki Giovanni and the New York Community Choir, Right On Records, RR95001.

[34]Breitman, *Malcolm X Speaks*, pp. 19-20.

[35]The Nation of Islam became the Billilian Community, which in turn became the World Community of Al Islam in the West, which in turn became the American Muslim Mission.

[36]Lomax, *To Kill a Black Man*, p. 170.

[37]*Autobiography of Malcolm X*, p. 428.

[38]Ibid., p. 421.

Chapter 10: A Little White Lie in the Name of Black Truth

[1]Augustine, *The City of God*, trans. Marcus Dods (New York: Random House, 1950), pp. 345-668.

[2]Robert Knudsen, *History* (Cherry Hill, N.J.: Mack, 1976), p. 15.
[3]Robert Knudsen, *The Secularization of Science* (Memphis, Tenn.: Christian Studies Center, 1954), pp. 8-9.
[4]Knudsen, *History*, p. 15.
[5]Knudsen, *Secularization of Science*, p. 9.
[6]Louis L. Knowles and Kenneth Prewill, eds., *Institutional Racism in America* (Englewood Cliffs, N.J.: Prentice-Hall, 1969), pp. 142-43.
[7]*Autobiography of Malcolm X*, p. 369, his emphasis.

Chapter 11: "Busting Out"

[1]Duke Ellington, "Something about Believing," *Second Sacred Concert*, Prestige, 1974, P-24045.
[2]Gerhard Kittel, ed., "κατέχω," in *Theological Dictionary of the New Testament*, trans. Geoffrey W. Bromiley, 10 vols. (Grand Rapids, Mich.: Eerdmans, 1964), 2:829.
[3]Osadolor Imasogie, "African Traditional Religion and Christian Faith," *Baptist Theological Journal* 70, no. 3 (Summer 1973):289-90.

Chapter 12: "That Boy Sho' Can Preach!"

[1]Miles Davis, "On Green Dolphin Street," *Basic Miles*, Columbia Records, YPC 32025.

Chapter 13: Cultural Seeding

[1]Marvin Gaye, *What's Going On?* Tamala Records, 1971, TS-310.
[2]Stevie Wonder, *Music of My Mind*, Tamala Records, 1972, T-314L; *Talking Book*, Tamala Records, 1972, T-319L; *Inner Visions*, Tamala Records, 1973, T-326L; *Fulfillingness First Finale*, Tamala Records, 1974, T-633251; *Songs in the Key of Life*, Tamala Records, 1976, T13-34062.
[3]Marvin Gaye, "Let's Get It On," *Let's Get It On*, Tamala Records, 1973, T-329V1.

Chapter 14: New Vistas

[1]W. A. Pratney, "Leadership Training Manual—Black Ministries Unlimited" (Los Angeles, 1975), p. 45, my emphasis.

Chapter 15: The Fields Are Black unto Harvest

[1]James Weldon Johnson, "Lift Every Voice and Sing," © Edward B. Marks Music Corporation. Used by permission.

Glossary

A'nt Jane.   (Aunt Jane) and/or Miss Sally. Usually the oldest or one of the oldest "mothers of the church." She has little or no formal education but she knows the Lord and has a homespun, God-given wisdom from life experience. She cannot articulate her faith intellectually, but she has discernment to know when ideas are not scriptural. Every traditional Black church has an A'nt Jane or a Miss Sally.

Black humanism.   A belief that Black people and Black cultural standards are the final authority of all truth, or that Blacks are not really affected by unrighteousness.

Blackness.   A perspective on reality based on the cultural consciousness (including sense of history and destiny) of Afro-American people.

Christianity.   The gospel applied in a cultural context, involving both its expression and the response of its adherents. These cultural manifestations do not contradict or undercut the gospel itself. On the contrary, when functioning properly a cultural Christianity can bring out insights on the gospel not seen in other cultural contexts.

Christianity-ism. (Or "Christianity" in quotation marks) This ugly term refers to negative unchristian religious practices expressed in the language of Christianity. The basis of Christianity-ism consists of making Christianity itself the *object* of faith rather than the expression of faith in God's solution to man's problem of human unrighteousness and God's revealed wrath on mankind. Christianity-ism in essence is a subtle form of idol worship—the idol being institutional Christianity, and the form often being associated with racism.

Consciousness or collective consciousness. That which a people uses to understand its world. Consciousness determines what people do and how they do it in every area of life. It also gives rise to a people's history and destiny as well as their sociology, psychology and anthropology.

Cultural dynamic. See Soul dynamic.

Culture. The cumulative effect of history, consciousness and destiny on the life of a collective body of people. Culture is made up of commitments, values and beliefs about the world and the people in it. The radical root of culture is the dynamic interplay between positive religious commitments (which are the result of God's grace) and negative religious commitments (which are the result of human unrighteousness). Culture results in the patterned way people do things together.

Destiny. A people's sense of the direction and ultimate fulfillment of their history.

Ethics. Concerning how we are to obey God. Ethics is not a branch of theology but equivalent to theology because all theology answers ethical questions.

Evangelicals. People who, like the fundamentalists, are associated with a belief in the so-called fundamentals of the faith (*see* Fundamentalists). But, unlike the fundamentalists, evangelicals generally have a broader view of culture and are a little more involved in cultural issues.

Existential. (Not existentialism) Dealing with the application of truth to the needs of the moment, understanding what it means in terms of the present situation.

Faith. The proper response to the gospel for which God holds every individual who hears it responsible. Faith is a reliance on God's grace alone for the solution to man's problem of unrighteousness and God's revealed wrath on mankind—a grace which is rooted in Christ. True faith is more than mere belief. It also includes (1) a complete turning away from unrighteousness and all attempts to solve man's problem with God by human means (repentance), and (2) a complete submission to Christ as supreme Lord and ultimate authority. In essence, faith is the root of righteousness.

Fundamentalists. People who are associated with a belief in the so-called fundamentals of the faith, including the inspiration and inerrancy of the Scriptures, the virgin birth of Christ, the deity of Christ, the atoning work of Christ on the cross, the physical return of Christ and so on. However, fundamentalists usually have a narrow view of culture and are generally not involved in cultural issues. Fundamentalists tend to emphasize personal salvation to the exclusion of the other aspects of the Great Commission.

Generic. The basic essence of an idea; that is, the basic underlying pattern of, for example, religion.

The Gospel. The good news that God through Christ has accomplished the solution to man's problem of unrighteousness and God's revealed wrath on mankind. The gospel reveals that God, by way of his Spirit, has delivered his people from his wrath and is developing in them the will and the power to pursue his righteousness. God applies this salvation by his grace through faith—faith which is a gift of God's grace (see Faith). In other words, the gospel tells us that God does transform those who properly respond to him from the practice of negative religion to positive religion.

Grace (God's grace). The unmerited favor of God toward man.

"Grace." (Always with quotation marks to distinguish it from God's grace) The world of God and the angels, that is, the "sacred" world which has little to do with the "secular" world.

History. A record of significant events of the past—events whose significance is determined by consciousness.

Islam-ism. Non-Islamic religious practices expressed in the language of Islam; for example, The Nation of Islam.

Liberalism. (Theological liberalism) A nineteenth-century movement which attempted to do theology without Scripture as a base. Liberalism was not bound by the teachings of orthodox theology such as the infallibility of the Scriptures, the deity of Christ or the sovereignty of God. According to liberalism, man's social progress will result in an ideal society. "Man come of age" became the rally phrase of liberalism early in the twentieth century. But the horrors of World War 1 shattered its optimistic assumptions. Today conservative Christians use this term to refer to those whose view of the authority of Scripture, the deity of Christ and the sovereignty of God is less strict than their own.

"Nature." The world of man and his environment, that is, the "secular" world which is independent from the "sacred" world.

Neo-orthodoxy. An early twentieth-century response to liberalism that affirmed many theological formulations which sounded more traditional and orthodox. In many cases this reaffirmed the centrality of the Bible for theological reflection. More conservative theologians dubbed the movement neo-orthodoxy because they believed that its adherents held an inadequate doctrine of revelation and thus yielded too much ground to modern critical theories of the Bible.

Reformed. A position associated with the classic creeds and confessions of the Reformation. While Reformed Christians essentially agree with fundamentalists and evangelicals in regard to the so-called fundamentals of the faith, they distinguish themselves from these other groups by their highly rational theological systems which deal with many aspects of life and culture. Reformed Christians are usually quick to point out that their theology is more consistent with the sovereignty of God than is the stance of their evangelical and fundamentalist counterparts. However, by and large this well-worked out view of the Great Commission remains for them theoretical; it has yet to be worked out in real life.

Righteousness. The perpetual pursuit of God and his revelation in every area of life both individually and corporately. It consists of seeking to live by the principles of the kingdom of God—principles that manifest themselves in qualities such as justice, equality, integrity, compassion, grace, love and so on. Righteousness is the fulfillment of godliness and liberation, and without the pursuit of righteousness neither godliness nor liberation is possible. Righteousness is also the fruit of faith.

Second exodus. The notion that Black history and Hebrew history have parallels. This is one of the basic motifs of historic Black theology. American slavery was seen in terms of Hebrew slavery in Egypt, and the White slavemasters were seen as Pharaoh. During slavery the North was seen as the temporal promised land, heaven as the eternal promised land. After the emancipation, the eternal promised land remained the same but the temporal promised land came to symbolize true freedom and human dignity. Our postslavery period has been seen as the wilderness wandering.

Soul dynamic. The core of Black culture which developed in the context of White oppression and Black resistance to oppression. This dynamic is a combination of two main components: (1) A theological dynamic—an oral tradition which emerged from the historic Black church experience. It captures nuggets of biblical truth in forceful, affective phrases and mental images out of life experience. (2) A cultural dynamic—deeply moving expressions of Black consciousness which emerge from the very roots of their humanity and experience, from levels where the image of God cannot be suppressed. Because they are aligned with the power of God's Word, these expressions have the power to deeply affect others who encounter them.

270.08
E471

Theological dynamic. *See* Soul dynamic.

Toning. Preaching in a musical tone. Toning is often accompanied by whooping in traditional Black preaching.

White humanism. A belief that White people and White cultural standards are the final reference point for all truth, or that Whites are not really affected by unrighteousness.

Whiteness. A perspective on reality based on the cultural consciousness (including sense of history and destiny) of Euro-American people.

Whooping. An abrupt gutteral sound that punctuates phrases in some traditional Black preaching. The whoop is a kind of oral exclamation point and is usually used in conjunction with toning.

3 4711 00172 6837